MIRELLA AMATO

Beeru

Everything you need to know to enjoy beer . . . even more

logy

appetite
by RANDOM HOUSE

Appetite by Random House® is a registered trademark of Random House LLC

Library and Archives of Canada Cataloguing in Publication is available upon request.

Print ISBN: 9780449016121

e-book ISBN: 9780449016138

Photography by Brilynn Ferguson and Elvis Deane

Photograph on page 45 © FLariviere/Shutterstock.com

Author photograph on pages x-xi by Alexa Clark

Printed and bound in China

Published in Canada by Appetite by Random House®,

a division of Random House of Canada Limited,

a Penguin Random House Company

www.randomhouse.ca

10 9 8 7 6 5 4 3 2

To

Lorenzo Dabove,

my beer *maestro,*

for his guidance and

unwavering support.

CONTENTS

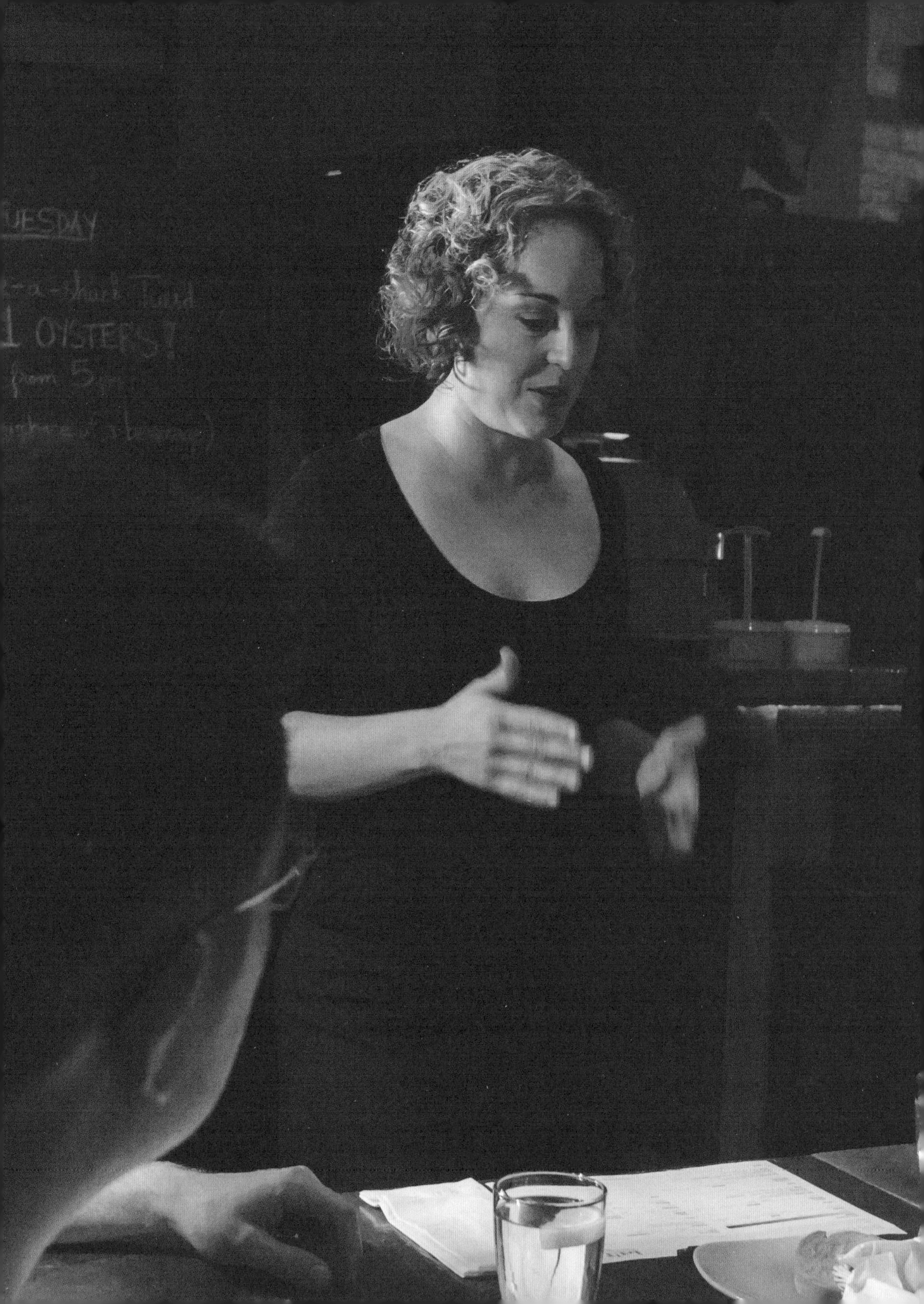
UESDAY
OYSTERS!
from 5

PEOPLE OFTEN ASK what drew me into the beer industry. The answer's simple: beer. It's delicious!

I've been a fan of beer for a very long time. It's enthralling in so many ways. Apart from being tasty, it is an amazingly varied and complex beverage; there's a beer for every mood, every food and every occasion. Some offer refreshment after work on a hot summer's day; others are rich and soothing when it's cold outside. Beer is equally at home in a sports bar as it is in a five-star restaurant. It's a beverage that is familiar to many, and yet it never ceases to surprise.

I discovered craft and imported beers early on, in my late teens, and I remember wondering why anyone would choose to always drink the same brand. I still regularly meet people who love to explore wine and food but haven't given much thought to beer and I am just as perplexed. Most people at least know whether it's best to serve red or white wine with a given dish. There are still far too many people who, if asked to pair the same dish with a beer, wouldn't know where to start. I hope they will start with this book.

This is my crusade: I want to live in a world where everyone has the same basic understanding and appreciation for beer as they do for wine.

A WORLD TO DISCOVER This book is for anyone with an inquisitive mind and an epicurean streak. It is a celebration of beer in its many delicious forms. It is an invitation to explore beer and seek out new favourites. I won't be offering lists of beers to try, because every beer is worth trying at least once. I'll share a few pointers, but won't presume to lay down the law about when or with what to drink which beer because everyone's palate and preferences are different.

In my years conducting guided beer tastings, I've learned that it often takes only a little information to turn curiosity into enthusiasm and set a beer novice on the path to becoming a connoisseur. I've also learned that because everyone's taste is different, each person makes a unique set of discoveries. At the end of my tastings, I often hold a show-of-hands vote asking which beers have come out on top. Inevitably the votes are split across the board, with each participant gravitating towards a different flavour, style, ingredient or historical tidbit. As a consequence, I've never felt that recommending specific beers is particularly useful. I'm not in the business of telling people what to drink. That's not what this book is about.

Instead, this book provides the basic information necessary to understand beer as a beverage, feel comfortable navigating a beer menu and zero in on personal preferences. It is an invitation to enter the world of beer and a guide to making the most of your journey there. It will provide tools and tips to assist you in exploring every aspect of beer, including styles and flavours, tasting—and hosting tasting parties—storage and service, food pairing and mixing beer cocktails.

Before we dive in, it is about time I, as your proposed guide, introduced myself.

WHY ME? When I first got into beer, I was often teased because I always wanted to go to "one of my fancy bars" in order to savour making a selection from a wide range of brands. I would drag friends out to breweries to learn more about beer and regularly monopolized pub staff in order to grill them for information. In short, I was (and still am) a bit of a beer geek.

The thought of turning my hobby and passion into full-time employment had always been in the back of my mind, but I wasn't sure how to make it happen. Then in 2007, I moved back to Canada after a year abroad, effectively abandoning my previous line of work, and decided to dive into beer and see where it might take me.

I'm curious by nature, love to learn, and have the certificates to prove it! I'm a National BJCP (Beer Judge Certification Program) judge. I completed the Certified Cicerone certification, which is a

Everything I do has a common goal: to cultivate and refine beer appreciation at all levels.

specialization in the selection, storage and service of beer, and in 2012 I became the first person outside the U.S.—and only the sixth person in North America—to earn the title of Master Cicerone. I've even dabbled in wine and spirits, completing the intermediate certificate with WSET (the Wine and Spirits Education Trust) in order to further hone my sensory evaluation skills.

I have essentially created my own job. I'm frequently asked why I don't start up my own brewery or pub. While I have indeed brewed beer and do work closely with both brewers and publicans, I can't imagine loving a job more than the one I have. It's easier to love than define. It has many facets, ranging from guided beer tastings and talking on the radio to training staff and consulting. Everything I do has a common goal: to cultivate and refine beer appreciation at all levels. The two greatest joys in my work are learning new things and sharing that knowledge with others. It is a privilege and a joy to introduce people to new beers or show them one they already know in a different light.

The world of beer is vast, with so many areas to explore, from ingredients and brewing to judging and styles, to history and traditions as well as proper handling, storage and service. It is also in constant evolution. New breweries, beer styles, brewing technologies and historical and scientific research are testing our definition of beer every day; keeping up with the latest trends and discoveries is an exhilarating challenge.

These past few years have been a fantastic experience. We are spoiled to live in a time when there is a phenomenal selection of readily available beers in so many styles and flavours. My journey exploring these beers has very much enriched my life as well as providing me with a living, and I delight in sharing my knowledge and enthusiasm for beer with others.

BEER SHOULD BE FUN! I'm often asked how I feel about the fact that beer isn't revered in the same way as wine and whether I feel that beer should be "elevated" to the same status. My answer is no. Beer and wine are both delicious and well worth exploring, but they are otherwise separate and distinct beverages. Still, beer definitely deserves a little more attention than it's currently getting.

It doesn't take extensive study to gain a much better appreciation for beer. After all, it's just beer; most of us are already quite familiar with it. All it takes is some basic information—you'll find it in the following pages—and a little attention. It's as easy as taking a second to stop and notice aromas and flavours and register how they resonate with you in that moment. It's as fun as throwing caution to the wind and trying the one beer on the menu that you've never heard of before. How are you going to discover your favourite beer if you've never tasted it?

It's true that beer doesn't have the best reputation. It's said to be fattening, which it isn't. Beer is fat-free and cholesterol-free and contains fewer calories than the equivalent amount of skim milk or juice (not to mention coolers and other alcoholic beverages). Some miss out on beer because they're under the mistaken impression that other alcoholic beverages are healthier when, in fact, beer is packed with vitamins and minerals. It also has probiotic qualities and contains a range of antioxidants.

Finally, there are those who shun beer, dismissing it as a party drink because of its association with binge drinking and hooliganism. This is another reason I'm crusading for a better understanding—and better enjoyment—of beer.

The good news is that learning about beer is easy and a lot of fun—as I'm sure readers of this book will find. Beer is effervescent and delicious; it is, at its root, a sociable beverage. It deserves to be studied and understood, but more important, it should be enjoyed and celebrated!

PART ONE

Beer Basics

TO GET THE MOST out of beer tasting, it's quite helpful to know what went into the beer in the first place. The colour, aroma, flavour and what we call mouthfeel can all be traced back to ingredients and brewing technique.

In a nutshell, beer is a cereal grain–based, fermented alcoholic beverage. A number of beverages fall into this broad category, but the one we most commonly associate with the term *beer* is a combination of water, malt, hops and yeast. Each of these four ingredients contributes something different, affecting how a beer looks, smells and tastes and the sensations it creates on the palate.

INGREDIENTS

Water Beer is over 90 percent water. The water used for brewing comes from a variety of sources, including natural springs, icebergs and glaciers, as well as local wells and taps. More important than the source of water, however, is its chemical composition; the pH level, hardness and mineral content of brewing water all affect the final beer. To avoid my delving into a lecture on chemistry, suffice it to say that the brewing process includes a series of chemical reactions that can only occur under certain conditions in a specific environment. Since that environment is essentially the water, its composition needs to be just right for the beer to be brewed successfully and attain its ideal flavour.

The composition of brewing water can also subtly influence a beer's colour, aroma, flavour and mouthfeel. In nineteenth-century Britain—to cite a classic example—the pale ales of Burton-upon-Trent were celebrated for being deliciously crisp and dry. We now know what was responsible: sulphates and calcium in the local water. Thanks to all that's been learned about water chemistry, brewers are now able to treat their water before working with it, to great effect. Brewers of pale

ale can—and frequently do—add sulphates, in the form of gypsum salts, to brewing water from anywhere in the world. This process is commonly referred to as *Burtonizing*.

Despite having chemical aids at their disposal, some brewers choose to use spring water or dechlorinated local tap water and focus on beer styles that work with their local water chemistry. Others prefer to filter and remineralize water in order to brew different styles and attain a specific flavour.

Malt This refers to barley that has been malted. Other grains can be malted, but will be referred to by name—for example, "malted wheat" or "malted rye." Because barley is the main cereal grain used in beer, the term *malt* has been adopted as shorthand.

Very few brewers malt their own grains. As a general rule, malting is a separate industry and brewers purchase their grains already malted. The malting process has two stages. The first is sprouting. Maltsters will wet and warm grains, encouraging them to sprout in order to trigger a chemical reaction (developing enzymes that will turn starches in the grain into sugars). Before the conversion takes place, maltsters will dry the malted grains, allowing the brewer to activate this conversion later, at the brewhouse.

Malted grains are dried in a kiln, which is a type of oven, and some of them are then roasted. Essentially, they are cooked. The degree of kilning and/or roasting will directly affect the colour of beer and contribute to its aroma and flavour. It's like toasting bread. A lightly toasted slice will retain its colour and taste like bread. Continue to toast, and the colour will darken and the flavours evolve and intensify until, eventually, the toast is burnt.

Hops The flowers of the hop plant contribute bitterness, aroma and flavour to beer. Hops also act as a natural preservative, which is why they are customarily included in beer recipes. Before their preservative properties were discovered, a variety of different herbs were used to

Hot Liquor in a Brewery?

In a brewery, the water that will be used to make beer is referred to as "liquor." This distinguishes it from the water in the brewery that will be used for cleaning or other purposes. It will often have been filtered or otherwise treated before being transferred into the hot liquor tank, where it will be heated up in preparation for brewing.

spice beer; these included horehound, sage, dandelion, nettle, gentian, clary sage and bogmyrtle. Nowadays, if a brewer chooses to eschew hops, and instead use a blend of herbs, the resulting beverage is referred to as *gruit*. This was historically the name given to the mix of herbs that a brewer would add to beer.

There are many different varieties of hops, each with its own distinct aroma and flavour. There's mint, lemon, grapefruit, mango, currants, gooseberry, eucalyptus, grass, flowers, pepper, garlic, onions and more. Each variety will also contribute a different level of bitterness to beer. Another interesting thing to note about hop varieties is that their character is affected by terroir—the particular land and climate in which they were grown. Transplanting a European hop variety to North America will result in a flower with a completely different character. In addition to this, new hop varieties are being created all the time through breeding programs. The American hops that have taken the beer world by storm, for example, were developed in the mid-twentieth century to have a bolder bitterness and bright aroma and flavour, which often includes striking citrus, tropical fruit or resin notes.

Hop flowers

Yeast Yeasts are microorganisms in the fungus family. During the fermentation phase of brewing, yeasts consume sugar and produce alcohol and carbon dioxide. Yeasts also release aroma and flavour compounds that can include fruity, spicy and buttery notes, among others (as well as, under certain conditions, some rather less pleasant ones). Like hops, yeasts are available in a variety of different strains, which are usually isolated and cultivated in labs. Most strains used for brewing fall either in the species of *Saccharomyces cervisiae* (ale yeast) or *Saccharomyces pastorianus* (lager yeast—a.k.a. *Saccharomyces carlsbergensis*).

These days, whether a beer is categorized as an ale or a lager depends on the strain used to brew it. Ale yeasts and Lager yeasts affect the flavour profile of a beer in different ways. Ale yeasts generally produce more esters, phenols and other flavour-making compounds, contributing additional complexity to beer. They also leave behind some sugars that will, on occasion, add sweetness to beer and also add to the body of the beer (for more on body, see 'mouthfeel' page 23). Lager yeasts ferment at a lower temperature than ale yeasts and take a lot more time. They will emit flavour compounds, but will then either reabsorb or break those compounds down in the later stages of fermentation (also known as conditioning), letting the malt and hop character shine through. In addition to this, lager yeasts can consume a wider range of sugars, resulting in a crisper beer.

Other yeasts and benign bacteria are used to ferment particular types of beer. See page 103 for more information on these ingredients.

THERE'S MORE?

The many other ingredients used in beer recipes can be divided into three categories:

Grains With the notable exception of gluten-free beer, the majority of beers are barley-based, with barley occupying a minimum of 30 percent of the grain bill and often quite a bit more. Other grains—in malted or unmalted form—can be used to make a beer's flavour more complex. Among them are wheat, rye, millet and buckwheat. Certain grains serve other purposes, such as helping promote a rich head of foam or enhancing mouthfeel.

Adjuncts An adjunct is any ingredient, apart from malted grain, that contributes fermentable sugars to beer. The most familiar examples are corn or corn syrup and rice. Some breweries use sugar, some molasses, others honey or maple syrup. Using a sugar to replace a portion of the grains results in a lighter body. Some adjuncts, like corn or rice, lighten the flavour, while others add complexity.

Flavouring Ingredients This is a very broad category. Brewers add all kinds of things to flavour beer. More traditional flavouring ingredi-

Brewers add all kinds of things to flavour beer . . . pretty much anything can (and has) gone into a brew.

ents include fruits, herbs and spices. Beyond that, there are beers brewed with wine, roses, bacon, tea, chocolate, cookies, oysters . . . pretty much anything can (and has) gone into a brew!

There is sometimes overlap between the second and third category here. For example, maple syrup is both an adjunct and a flavouring ingredient. You could say the same of fruits if they are added before fermentation because their sugars will then be consumed by the yeast. This is one of the reasons why some fruit beers are sweet while others aren't.

Finally, there is barrel aging, which can be seen as both a process and a flavouring ingredient (see page 102 for more on this). In some cases, brewers will acquire wood chips that were first designed for wine and use them to contribute a barrel-aged flavour to beer without having to purchase and accommodate wooden barrels.

Brew House

BREWING

Now it's time to bring all the ingredients together. Water, malted barley, hops and yeast (and sometimes other ingredients) have to be combined through a series of specific, carefully controlled steps in order to become beer. The brewing process is designed to extract particular components from each ingredient in order to achieve the ideal colour, aroma, flavour, bitterness, alcohol content and mouthfeel in the finished product. While the process varies, the basic steps in brewing are consistent and quite straightforward. Nevertheless, a brewer's job involves a lot of precision work, troubleshooting and continuous sanitation. The following explanation covers the broad strokes and will provide a basic understanding of the process, but is not meant as a guide to brewing. Those interested in home brewing will find suggested reading on page 164.

The Mash In this first step of the brewing process, the malted grains are steeped in water that has been heated to a specific temperature in order to activate a chemical reaction that will convert their starches into sugars. The mash temperature can be adjusted in stages so as to coax different enzymes into changing the composition of the mash and produce varying amounts of fermentable and unfermentable sugars. Fermentable sugars will be converted into alcohol by the yeast while unfermentable sugars will still be present in the finished product, contributing body and sometimes a light sweetness.

The Lauter Once the mash is finished and all of the starches have turned into sugar and dissolved into the water, it is time to get rid of the grain husks. The brewer will draw out the sugar water, known as wort (pronounced "wirt," like "dirt"), through a screen at the bottom of the vessel and the grain husks that accumulate on the screen serve as a filter. Once most of the wort has been drawn off, the brewer carefully runs additional water over the grains to extract as many sugars as possible. This is called *sparging*.

The Boil Wort is then transferred into a kettle to boil for at least one hour. Boiling serves many purposes, including condensing the wort as well as killing bacteria and wild yeasts. It is also during this phase that hops are added, traditionally in three stages. The hops that are added early will boil for a long time, allowing their bittering resins to dissolve into the beer. A second, "flavouring hop" addition is incorporated thirty to forty minutes before the end of the boil. These hops don't boil long enough to contribute a significant amount of bitterness to the beer. A third batch is then added moments before the end of the boil. These hops contribute aromatic essential oils, which are quite volatile and would be lost if boiled longer. Brewers can vary their hopping schedule in many ways to toggle the amount of hop bitterness, flavour and aroma in the final product. This is why some beers have a bold hop aroma and very little bitterness or vice versa.

Fermentation Wort is cooled to the proper temperature and transferred to a fermentation vessel where yeast is added. Because yeast is a living organism, throwing it into the boiling liquid would be disastrous.

What about the Gunk?

When pouring out a bottle-conditioned beer, it's a good idea to do so gently, leaving the sediment at the bottom. Having said this, some people do enjoy the added bite that the sediment adds. When trying a new bottle-conditioned beer, why not drink half without the yeast and then add the yeast to the remaining beer and decide which tastes better? When pouring for others, though, always leave the yeast in and bring them the bottle so that they can decide whether or not to pour in the sediment. It's important to note that unfiltered wheat beers will sometimes drop clear in the bottle. These beers are actually meant to be cloudy and the sediment should gently be mixed back in either before or during the pour.

During fermentation, yeast consumes the sugar in the wort, releasing alcohol and carbon dioxide. Essentially, it is the yeast that transforms wort into beer. The brewer can make various adjustments, choosing a specific yeast strain or altering the length and temperature of fermentation, for example, to encourage (or discourage) the production of particular aromas and flavours in the beer.

Packaging Once it is ready, the beer is filtered and carbonated. These steps are optional. Some brewers choose to capture and retain the carbonation created during the fermentation process. Others will add carbonation to the finished beer to reach a specific level. In addition to leaving beer clear, filtration also helps with stability and shelf life. Some breweries filter roughly, others use an additional microfiltration, and some breweries will choose to pasteurize. Once the beer is ready, it is packaged into bottles, cans or kegs.

An alternate way to serve beer is cask-conditioned. Cask-conditioned beer is drawn directly from the fermenter and packaged into a cask without being filtered or force-carbonated. The beer finishes conditioning in the cask, where yeast will consume the sugar that's left in the wort and carbonate naturally. The resulting beer is flavourful but delicate.

Similarly, some breweries bottle-condition their beer. This is made evident by a small layer of sediment at the bottom of the bottle made up, in part, of yeast that has carbonated the beer in the bottle before settling to the bottom.

Bottle conditioning at the brewery

STORAGE

Beer inevitably degrades over time. On occasion, a beer will spoil and become sour, but more often the flavours in a beer will become dull and lifeless as it stales, making way for unpleasant musty or cloying notes. How long an individual beer will keep depends on a number of factors including its alcohol content (alcohol being a natural preservative) as well as how it was brewed and packaged. Storing a beer properly will help ensure that it stays fresh as long as possible. Apart from the passing of time, there are three things that will damage beer and cause its flavours to stale more quickly: heat, oxygen and light.

Heat Because the degradation of beer is essentially a series of chemical reactions, exposure to heat will accelerate the process. Always store beer at a cool temperature, preferably in a cellar or fridge.

Oxygen Contact with oxygen also precipitates staling. Brewing, packaging and serving beer with as little oxygen contact as possible are the brewer and publican's responsibilities.

Light Exposing beer to light can do more than accelerate staling. It triggers a lightstruck reaction in the beer, resulting in an unpleasant skunk-like note. Light exposure is less of a concern with kegged or canned beer because these containers block the light. This also holds true for very dark beers, as the beers themselves block light. Green and clear bottles, however, leave beer vulnerable; they should be packaged and stored in a closed container and kept away from light.

CELLARING

Maintaining a beer cellar is a great way to add another dimension to beer appreciation. As a general rule, beers are ready to drink when they are released by the brewery; brewers will sometimes age a beer for months or even years before releasing it. While many beers are best enjoyed fresh and will deteriorate with age, some benefit from aging, developing new, complex flavours such as toffee, sherry or port, dried-fruit, and umami.

Which Beers to Cellar As a general rule, the best candidates are those with an alcohol content of at least 7% alcohol by volume (ABV). Some lighter-alcohol beers do age quite interestingly, however, and sour beers at any alcohol level also tend to age well. So do bottle-conditioned beers, because they still contain live yeast, which absorbs oxygen and protects the beer. On occasion, a brewer will indicate that a beer is ideal for cellaring by stating so on the label or clearly indicating the year, or vintage, on the bottle. Here are a few things to keep in mind when selecting beers to keep in the cellar:

- *Hop character will fade.* If hop aromas and flavours are the main feature in a beer, it's better to drink it fresh. If, however, hops are only one element in a beer's flavour profile, aging that beer will allow other flavours to come forward.
- *Aging causes flavours to meld together, and eventually, deeper flavours will emerge.* If a beer displays a range of distinct, strong flavours and aromas, or presents sharp alcohol notes, aging it will refine its character and lend elegance to the beer.
- *As beer ages, it becomes drier.* When sharper notes fade, malt tones become prominent, often developing notes of sweet toffee, molasses or sherry. With further aging, the beer thins out, and deeper notes of leather, almond, coffee, dried-fruit, soy or umami often emerge. Therefore, a beer with a rich, chewy, malty character will generally age more interestingly than one that is very dry (with the exception of sour beers).

My Beer is Skunky!

Many people use the term *skunky* to describe any beer that is off, when, in fact, it's a specific term. When beer is exposed to light, dissolved components from the hops break down, resulting in compounds that are almost identical to those that come out of the scent glands of a skunk.

The best way to know if a beer's flavours will evolve interestingly over time is to cellar it and try it in a year or so. Whether the results are positive or negative, they are always informative.

How to Cellar Beer Beer should be cellared in a location with a cool, consistent temperature (10–13°C, or 50–55°F). Exposure to light should be avoided and it is best to put clear or green bottles in sealed boxes (or, preferably, keep them in the box in which they were packaged). Beers should be stored standing up in order to minimize potential oxygen exposure and to keep the liquid away from the cap, which might become damaged over time, imparting unwanted flavours to beer. Here are a few additional tips:

Beer aging at the brewery before its release

- *Be organized.* Make sure to put a sticker or label on each beer with the date and any other pertinent information that will help to identify it later. Keep and update a list of the beers that are in the cellar. Bottles can pile up quickly and it's easy to forget the ones that are sitting at the back of the shelf.
- *When cellaring a new beer for the first time, buy at least three bottles.* The first should be consumed right away to assess whether it's worth aging. It's also a good idea to take tasting notes to compare later with those for the aged version. The second bottle should be opened after a year or so. Depending on how the second beer has evolved, the third one can either be consumed right away or aged for another while.
- *Aged beers also make fantastic gifts,* by the way.

SERVING TEMPERATURE The temperature at which a beer is served will affect our appreciation of its flavours. As a general rule, malt flavours and yeast character are muted in a colder beer, highlighting its hop character. Beer also retains more carbonation at lower temperatures. As beer warms, carbonation is released and a greater complexity emerges. While cold beer is definitely more refreshing, the more complex and flavourful the beer, the warmer the temperature at which it should be served. As a general guideline, crisp, refreshing beers, like those in the Refreshing Brews chapter of this book, can be consumed right out of the fridge, while more complex beers should be pulled out of the fridge twenty to thirty minutes before drinking. Higher-alcohol beers tend to be quite complex and should be stored in a cellar or pulled out of the fridge an hour before they are to be consumed.

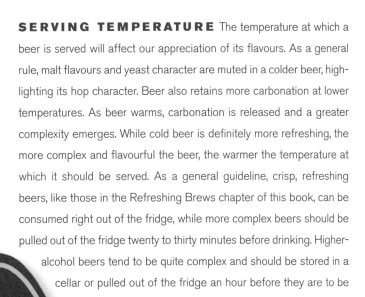

CHOOSING GLASSWARE The glass a beer is served in can also have an effect. Beer glasses come in many shapes. Some, like the pilsner or Weissbier glass, are closely linked with a specific beer style. Others, like the ubiquitous nonic pint glass, seem to have a more general use.

While some features of a glass will enhance a beer's appearance, carbonation levels, flavour, aroma and colour, it's not strictly necessary to have a different glass for each particular beer. A set of three will cover the majority of beer styles. Here is a breakdown of the three basic beer-glass shapes and how each of them complements its content.

Wide Glass This is perhaps the most common style. In this category are the nonic pint, the tulip pint and the shaker pint, among others. What these glasses have in common is a wide base, wide body and wide lip. Their generous proportions are best suited to lower-alcohol beers, up to 7% ABV—for example, amber and dark ales; porters and stouts and pale ales. The wide rim is great for complex, fuller-flavoured beers in that alcohol range, because there is a lot of surface area to allow aromas to come through. The wider glass also allows for more carbonation to be released, which will help bring those aromas up to the nose. The wide lip is designed to splay the beer across the tongue, distributing it to various taste receptors and allowing the nose to enter the glass and capture aromas as the beer is sipped.

Narrow Glass This group, which includes both the pilsner and Weiss-bier glasses noted above, is ideal for light, crisp, refreshing beers (up to 7% ABV). Being taller as well as narrow, these glasses carry the same volume as the wide variety. The slender shape is designed to show off a paler colour by allowing light to shine through. It is also designed to hold carbonation, much like a champagne flute, and is

Scratch 'n Sniff

Some glasses have patterns etched onto the inside of their base. This etching is designed to release carbonation, bringing more aromas to the nose and replenishing the foam head. The etching causes nucleation sites that will encourage carbonation to break out of solution. While this technique does enhance a beer's appearance and aroma at first, it will also cause it to become flat more quickly.

ideal for beer styles with bold carbonation. Highly carbonated beer styles also tend to present a full head of foam, which the tall narrow walls of this glass will help to support. The narrower opening will concentrate delicate aromas and the tall shape of the glass is designed for big swigs, shooting the beer to the back of the throat.

Stemmed Glass Stemmed beer glasses come in three basic rounded shapes—a snifter, a tulip and a chalice. They also tend to hold a lower volume, which helps moderate the consumption of higher-alcohol beers such as abbey and Trappist ales. Like the wide glass, they all have a wide lip that allows complex flavours and aromas to be savoured. The rounded shape is ideal for swirling to release aromas. It also allows you to comfortably cup the beer in your hands and warm it, if necessary.

THE PROPER POUR Having stored the beer carefully, made sure it's at the correct temperature and selected the right glass, there is one last step for a delightful beer experience: the proper pour. This may seem like a bit of a production at first, requiring some focus and concentration, but it quickly becomes second nature. There are some beer styles and brands that have specific pouring techniques associated with them and these can be fun to master. Having said this, here is a universal pouring technique that will help bring out the best in any beer:

- *Rinse the glass with cold water.* It's always a good idea to give the glass a quick cold-water rinse if there is a sink nearby. The rinse serves two purposes. First, it gets rid of any dust or dishwasher residue. If left in the glass, these will cause the formation of tiny bubbles along the inside of the glass and serve as nucleation sites (see sidebar on page 17). Rinsing also chills the glass, which prevents beer from foaming too much and assists with a smoother pour.
- *Start the pour.* Hold the glass at a 45-degree angle. The bottle should hover above the glass, its lip staying about an inch above the rim. Start pouring the beer gently onto the inside wall of the glass. This minimizes foaming.
- *Straighten the glass.* Once the glass is just over half full, start straightening it and pour directly into the centre. This releases carbonation and forms head. Depending on how carbonated the beer is, it may be necessary to straighten the glass earlier or a bit later to get the ideal amount of foam.

Frozen Glassware

It is not necessary to freeze beer glassware. Rinsing a room-temperature glass with cold water will bring it to the right temperature. When a glass has been in the freezer, it is equally important to rinse it with cold water. This will bring it up to the right temperature for pouring because a frozen glass will cause foaming. It's also important to be aware that glassware can pick up unpleasant odours if it has been sitting in a freezer for a while—odours that will then transfer to the beer.

• **_Leave some foam!_** Once the pour is complete, there should be about two fingers of foam, or the diameter of a quarter resting on the beer. It's important to note that brewers plan for their beer to be poured properly. To compensate for the carbon dioxide released during the pour, they slightly overcarbonate. A beer poured without foam will not only display fewer aromas, it can also cause an uncomfortably full feeling.

BEER IS AN EVERYDAY beverage and can certainly be enjoyed as such, simply adding conviviality to a friendly gathering. Taking time to really taste it, however, will open the door to a whole different level of enjoyment. This can be as simple as pausing for a moment to nose the beer and then linger on the first sip. Doing so reveals a complexity of flavour, making every beer a rewarding experience. The more a beer is examined, the more it reveals. In the context of a formal beer tasting, it is helpful to have some technique.

This chapter outlines basic beer-tasting technique, and different details to look for. The *Beerology* tasting sheet (see pages 156–157) provides helpful guidelines and terminology. It can also be downloaded from the Beerology.ca website, printed and shared with guests during a guided beer tasting, or used to record personal impressions when sampling a new beer.

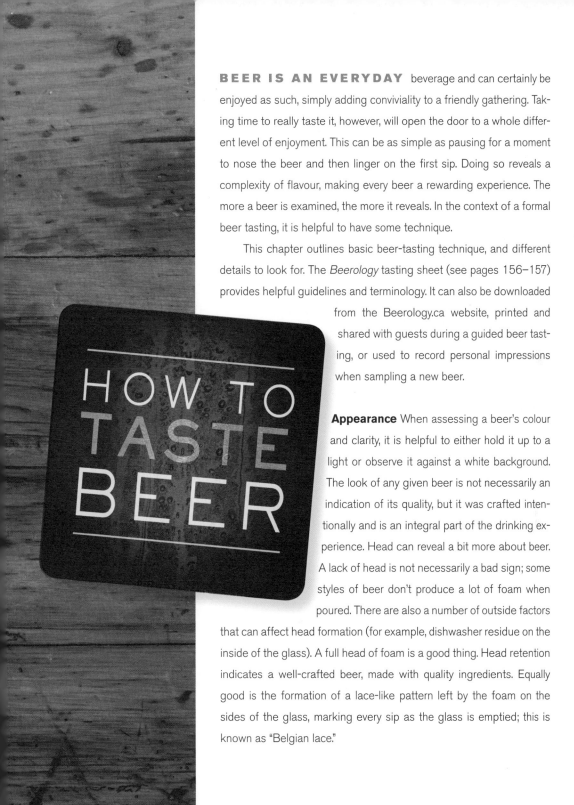

HOW TO TASTE BEER

Appearance When assessing a beer's colour and clarity, it is helpful to either hold it up to a light or observe it against a white background. The look of any given beer is not necessarily an indication of its quality, but it was crafted intentionally and is an integral part of the drinking experience. Head can reveal a bit more about beer. A lack of head is not necessarily a bad sign; some styles of beer don't produce a lot of foam when poured. There are also a number of outside factors that can affect head formation (for example, dishwasher residue on the inside of the glass). A full head of foam is a good thing. Head retention indicates a well-crafted beer, made with quality ingredients. Equally good is the formation of a lace-like pattern left by the foam on the sides of the glass, marking every sip as the glass is emptied; this is known as "Belgian lace."

Aroma Aroma is perhaps the most important element in beer tasting. Our sense of smell informs taste, opening up a complexity of flavours to the palate. If a beer has no discernible aroma, swirling it around in the glass might help. This releases some carbonation, which carries aromas up to the nose. If the beer is very cold, warming it also helps to open up some of the aromas. Aroma is best captured in short spurts; after prolonged nosing, your senses may have adapted to the point where some of the aromas can't be discerned. When assessing aroma, it is always easiest to start with a general impression: How intense is the aroma? Is it sweet, sharp or a balance of different notes? From there, additional time can be spent identifying specifics.

Flavour Flavour should be a natural continuation of the aroma. A few added dimensions will appear, most notably bitterness and sometimes a sour note. Each sip can be swirled around the mouth before swallowing, helping you identify a broader range of flavours as there are nuances in how different parts of the mouth perceive flavour. This will also warm the beer, releasing carbonation and aromas. Once this is done, the beer should be swallowed because finish and aftertaste are key components in a beer's flavour profile. Having swallowed the beer, taking a few relaxed breaths through the nose with a closed mouth can reveal further nuances thanks to the stimulation of retronasal olfaction. Again, it is helpful to note the intensity of the flavour, the balance between sweetness and bitterness, and general impressions.

The "weight" of beer can vary from light to thick and chewy.

Mouthfeel Another component of beer tasting is mouthfeel, which describes the texture and weight of beer, as opposed to its actual flavour. High-alcohol beer can have a warming quality, not unlike hard alcohol, while bitter beers can sometimes be astringent. The weight, or body, of beer can also vary from light and watery to thicker and heavy or chewy. Something else to note is the carbonation level, since it varies between different beers: Is the level of carbonation pleasant or distracting?

Finish The final component of flavour is finish. This is observed by taking pauses between sips. The finish may be long, with lingering flavours, or short, with the beer disappearing immediately after it is swallowed. The aftertaste can be sweet or bitter, and can take on many flavours, either in succession or all at once. The intensity of the finish will vary, depending on the style of beer at hand. No matter how a beer finishes, it should leave the drinker wanting to take another sip.

General Impression It is always a good idea to synthesize everything that's been observed about a beer: Were the flavours lively and well balanced, or did they fall flat? Was there an aspect or flavour in particular that stood out? Did the beer have a fresh quality to it, or is it possible that it might have been stale? In addition to this, noting personal preference for future reference is always worthwhile.

PART TWO

Beer Styles

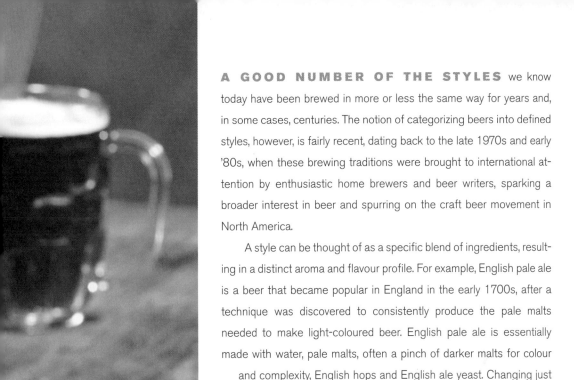

A GOOD NUMBER OF THE STYLES we know today have been brewed in more or less the same way for years and, in some cases, centuries. The notion of categorizing beers into defined styles, however, is fairly recent, dating back to the late 1970s and early '80s, when these brewing traditions were brought to international attention by enthusiastic home brewers and beer writers, sparking a broader interest in beer and spurring on the craft beer movement in North America.

A style can be thought of as a specific blend of ingredients, resulting in a distinct aroma and flavour profile. For example, English pale ale is a beer that became popular in England in the early 1700s, after a technique was discovered to consistently produce the pale malts needed to make light-coloured beer. English pale ale is essentially made with water, pale malts, often a pinch of darker malts for colour and complexity, English hops and English ale yeast. Changing just one or two of these ingredients will propel this beer into a different style category. Use characteristic West Coast U.S. hops instead of British ones and the beer becomes an American-style pale ale. Substitute darker malts and it might then be categorized as English brown ale.

Traditional beer styles evolved based on the ingredients available in different regions and on factors such as water quality, local palates, history and laws. While this chapter provides some history, its focus is on giving an overview of the style itself, an insight into its flavour and suggestions for how it might best be enjoyed. Beer history is fascinating; that's for another book entirely!

Ingredients are portable these days, meaning brewers all over the world can make whatever regional beer they like, and they certainly do! English-style pale ale, for instance, is not necessarily brewed in England. Defining traditional styles is a way to ensure that these are not lost as brewers revive them and experiment with ingredients and techniques.

When shopping for beer, familiar brand names may be reassuring and funny names can be intriguing, but understanding which flavours to expect from the style declared on the label is a much more effective way to ensure you enjoy the contents. It's also important to note that not all beers are brewed according to a specific style. Sometimes brewers bring together a whole new set of ingredients and release a beer without a style name. This can be a delightful gustatory adventure.

There are sixty-two beer styles listed in this section. In some cases, the style categories listed are not traditional ones, but rather a grouping of styles with shared traits. Style guidelines were originally designed for home brewers and beer judges, while this book is for the consumer. Some styles with similar flavours have therefore been grouped together.

The list that follows is by no means comprehensive, but rather focuses on the most common styles available on the North American market. Many less common traditional styles that have been omitted from this section are briefly addressed in the glossary at the back of the book.

The Beerology Quadrant

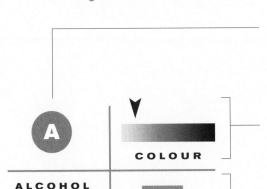

On most of the beer style pages you will see a quadrant of key information in the bottom corner. This will tell you four things at a glance:

Ale vs. Lager: which family of beers this style belongs to. Some are hybrids; some can be brewed as one or the other; and a rare few styles don't fit into either category.

A ALE   **L** LAGER

Colour: the colour you can expect this beer style to be, ranging from straw to black.

Distinct Taste: indicates specific tastes that can be pronounced in this style of beer, as follows:

B BITTER   **So** SOUR   **Sw** SWEET

A boldly coloured icon means that the distinct taste will definitely be there whereas a pale icon indicates that it might be present, depending on the individual brand.

Alcohol: the expected alcohol content for this style. For the purposes of this book, middle-range alcohol content is 4%–6% ABV.

You will not see this information for Fruit and Spiced Beer or in the Brews Beyond chapter. This is because the characteristics of the beers in those sections vary too greatly to be categorized.

Comparisons of different styles are also shown in a range of charts starting on page 159, at the back of the book. These can be used as a visual reference for the various traits, showing how styles compare to one another.

THE BEERS IN THIS CHAPTER may be contrasting in character but they all have one thing in common: they're designed for refreshment. Their refreshing nature can be linked to two shared traits. First, they all are relatively low in alcohol, allowing for better hydration. Also, the vast majority of the beers I've classified as "refreshing brews" are highly carbonated. When carbonation dissolves into a beer, it becomes carbonic acid, contributing a crisp, zesty acidity.

All of these beers are pale in colour—only a narrow selection of lighter-coloured grains can be used to brew them. These lightly cooked grains result in delicate, straightforward malt notes of fresh cereal grain or bread. A deeper character derived from a more complex blend of darker malts might distract from the refreshing qualities of these beers.

These are go-to styles for cottage and beach season. They are ideal for patio drinking or as a revitalizing reward after a workout. They pair well with delicate foods like salads, sandwiches and light appetizers.

Refreshing
BREWS

Golden Lagers

At a Glance Pale to deep gold in colour and crystal clear, these lagers have an alcohol content in the lower range and are designed to be approachable and refreshing. Their aromas and flavours are generally crisp and straightforward.

Overview This is the most popular style of beer in North America by far, dominating sales in both Canada and the U.S. Most people have tried at least one or two examples and may have preconceived notions about the style and whether they like it. The world of golden lagers is vast and nuanced, however. There are breweries of all sizes, in various parts of the world, striving to put their own signature on this ubiquitous style.

Golden lagers are ideal in moments when beer is not the focal point, but rather a pleasant accompaniment to other activities; they are conceived as "easy-drinking" beverages that allow the drinker to consume a few back to back over a period of time without developing palate fatigue.

Common Lager

Light in flavour, the character of common lager combines a soft sweetness and bold carbonation, with usually little or no hop bitterness in their finish. Some breweries release fuller-flavoured versions, with a more noticeable malt character and a detectable bitterness, still with a straightforward, accessible flavour profile.

The common lager emerged during the nineteenth century, when, thanks to improved transportation and communication in the wake of the Industrial Revolution, the rest of the world discovered the golden, crisp lagers that had taken Europe by storm. In addition to this, the advent of artificial refrigeration made it possible to brew lager beer anywhere. While international lagers were likely originally brewed in a traditional fashion, recipes were eventually adapted to make use of local ingredients and please local palates. Nowadays, a number of lager-focused breweries have become household names. These breweries spend a lot of time and resources in research and development as they endeavour to create crowd-pleasing beers.

Many common-lager recipes include adjuncts, such as rice, corn or syrup, in order to lighten the colour, body and flavour of the beer. Traditionally, however, these ingredients served another purpose. When European brewers first came to North America, they found that the barley that was commonly available here was not producing the same results as the barley they were using in Europe. The local variety had smaller kernels, with less starch to turn into sugar. These smaller kernels also meant more husks in the brew and the increased percentage of husks added harsh tannic notes to the final product. In order to adjust for this discrepancy and brew a more pleasant beer, a supplementary source of starch had to be found. Corn, being a common and accessible crop at the time, provided an obvious solution to this problem.

Fun for: Last-minute meals

Pairs with: Classic light-flavoured American foods, like hot dogs

Also labeled: Lager, Lager Beer, Premium Lager, Blonde Lager, Craft Lager, Session Lager, American-Style Lager, Domestic Lager, Pre-Prohibition Lager

Examples: Beach Blonde, Tree Brewing Co., CAN; Molson Canadian, CAN; Moosehead Lager, CAN; Pabst Blue Ribbon, USA; Session Premium Lager, Full Sail Brewing Co., USA

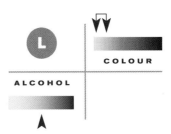

Lite Lager

Lite lagers are pale gold or straw-coloured and are similar to the common lager in their balance of flavours. They are, however, lighter in almost all aspects except for their carbonation level, which tends to be quite bold.

Developed in the U.S., the original lite lager, Gablinger's Diet Beer, was introduced by Rheingold of Brooklyn in 1967. The brand did not fare particularly well, but the Miller Brewing Company picked up the style and supported it with a classic advertising campaign using the slogan "Great Taste ... Less Filling!" Miller Lite's subsequent rise to popularity in the 1970s is credited with setting the lite lager on its path towards becoming the top-selling style of beer in North America.

The bold carbonation level in lite lagers balances the delicate, slightly sweet flavour by contributing a sharp bite in the finish. Strong carbonation also adds texture and volume to these otherwise very light-bodied beers. Lite lagers are lower in calories and often lower in their carbohydrate content.

Fun for: Day-long events

Pairs with: Extremely light-flavoured foods, like chips and dip

Also labeled: Light Lager, Light

Examples: Brewhouse Light, Great Western Brewing Co., CAN; Coors Light, USA; Cracked Canoe Premium Light Lager, Moosehead Breweries Ltd., CAN; Miller Lite, USA; Sam Adams Light, USA

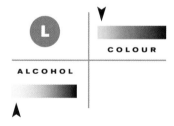

Pilsner

The vast majority of pilsners are all-malt beers. When compared to the previous beers in this chapter, another salient difference is the level of hopping, which gives pilsners a bitter finish.

Pilsner means "from Plzen," a town that is now part of the Czech Republic. This style pre-dates common and lite lagers; in fact, it inspired them. It is estimated that the pilsner has influenced over 90 percent of the beer available in the world today.

A young Bavarian brewer named Josef Groll first brewed the brand that made pilsners famous in 1842. He had come to Plzen to brew at a large new cutting-edge facility. There, he combined two key elements: lager yeast, which was gaining quite a reputation for the clean, crisp character that it gave; and British malting technology, which made it easier to consistently achieve a golden colour. The resulting beer was a hit and word spread fast, with brewers all over Europe and North America quickly adopting the style. Groll's beer was later re-named Pilsner Urquell, meaning "original source of the pilsner."

As the style spread, variations emerged, with brewers choosing to use local ingredients. Three often-cited subcategories are Bohemian, or Czech pilsner; German pilsner; and pre-Prohibition American-style pilsner.

Local hops provide distinct notes in each substyle. Bohemian pilsner traditionally uses a Czech hop called Saaz, which imparts delicate spicy notes, while the German one uses local hop varieties with more of an earthy or woodsy tone. The kind of hop in the American-style differs; brewers use either European hops or classic North American varieties.

Malt-wise, pre-Prohibition American-style pilsners are usually supplemented with rice or corn while their European counterparts are not. Because of the quality of the local water and malts available, pilsner brewers in what is now the Czech Republic had to boil sections of the mash in order to extract enough sugar from it, resulting in a slightly darker beer with a bit more body. Meanwhile, the mineral content in the water used to brew German pilsners contributed a dry mouthfeel, accenting their crisp bitter finish.

Fun for: Cooling down during summer days by the water

Pairs with: Light-flavoured fried foods, like deep-fried calamari

Also labeled: Pilsner

Examples: Bohemian Style Pilsener, Propeller Brewing Co., CAN; Pilsner Urquell, CZE; Sunshine Pils, Tröegs Brewery, USA; Steam Whistle Pilsner, CAN; Trumer Pils, Trumer Brauerei, USA

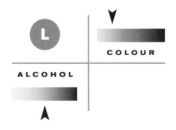

Munich Helles

Like its North American counterparts, this lager style from Munich is crisp with an accent on malt flavour and aroma. It is brewed without corn, rice, or syrup however, and its malt character is generally more pronounced. The malt usually comes across as a slight sweetness with fresh cereal grain or breadcrumb notes. The Helles is not as aggressively carbonated as North American lagers. It has a low but detectable hop bitterness in the finish, which is often accompanied by the delicate earthy or herbal hop aroma and flavour of German hops.

Oktoberfest Lager

A lager from Munich with an alcohol content around 6% ABV. It is medium-bodied and is designed for volume drinking, balancing rich cereal grain flavours with a moderate bitterness. The style we now know as Oktoberfest lager emerged at the Munich Oktoberfest in the mid-1900s as an alternative to the Märzen style (see page 49), which had been the beer of choice at the festival for years. By the late 1900s the golden option had become the official Oktoberfest beer style. In Europe, the term *Oktoberfestbier* is protected and can only be used by six large Munich-area breweries.

Also labeled: Oktoberfest Bier, Oktoberfestbier, Wiesn Bier, Festbier

Golden Ales

At a Glance Like their lager counterparts, golden ales are designed to be crisp and refreshing. They are not generally meant to inspire lengthy consideration. Some of these golden ales are, in fact, so similar to golden lagers that they are confused with them.

Overview While their flavour profile is still understated, golden ales generally do have a little more complexity than their lager counterparts. These beers also tend to be a tad darker in colour, moving into a deep gold.

Golden ales, like the lagers, are meant to be "easy-drinking" beers. They are a great style for golden lager drinkers to venture into when looking for a little more depth of flavour. Because these ales are not as dry as their counterparts, and have a light fruitiness, golden ales might also appeal to drinkers who generally enjoy dry sparkling ciders and wines.

Common Ale

Common ales are clear, crisp, golden beers brewed with an ale yeast. As a result, they can have a little more body than golden lagers, depending on whether or not adjuncts were used. Golden ales also have a little more sweetness and a hint of fruit or spice in the aroma and flavour—often a red or golden apple or pepper.

The common-ale category is a broad one, and it encompasses a range of beers being brewed around the world. They are clear and highly carbonated and their colour can range from pale to deep gold or occasionally amber. Like their lager counterparts, common ales are in some cases brewed with added rice, corn or syrup. With common ales, sometimes a percentage of wheat is also used. Closer scrutiny of common ales will reveal subtle differences and a little more complexity. Their aroma and flavour can include a light sweetness or biscuit note from the malt as well as a hint of fruit or spice that results from the use of ale yeast. The level of bitterness varies but is generally quite subtle and on occasion, imperceptible. These beers are light-bodied with a bold carbonation, which can add a crisp bite to the finish.

Fun for: Waiting at the bar

Pairs with: Bar snacks, like salted peanuts

Also labeled: Ale, Golden Ale, Export Ale, Domestic Ale, Blonde Ale, Summer Ale

Examples: Boréale Blonde, Les Brasseurs du Nord, CAN; Firemans #4 Blonde Ale, Real Ale Brewing Co., USA; Gold, Heavy Seas, USA; Labatt 50, CAN; Steelhead Extra Pale Ale, Mad River Brewing Co., USA

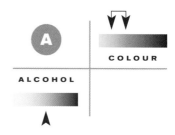

Cream Ale

Cream ale can be seen as a subcategory of the common ale. Beers in this group are clear and golden, with a lively carbonation. Cream ales are brewed with traditional North American malts supplemented by corn or rice. They have a detectable bitterness in the finish. Their aromas and flavours are quite subtle and combine to create a sweet, grainy character with hints of creamed corn and, on occasion, a slight fruitiness.

The cream ale style originated in North America and was popular and widespread before the days of Prohibition. It was born of necessity; brewers who didn't have refrigeration equipment were trying to make the most lager-like beer possible to compete with the popularity of pilsner-style beer. It is worth noting that modern cream ales are sometimes brewed with lager yeast or with a combination of yeasts. This style is often described as a hybrid, rather than an ale.

Note: Visitors who order a cream ale in the Canadian provinces of Québec and British Columbia may be perplexed to find that they are served a beer that does not at all fit the traditional description of the style. In Québec, the term *cream ale* sometimes describes a pale ale served on a nitrogen tap (see page 62). In British Columbia, it can point to a reddish-brown beer resembling a dark, English mild.

Both of these quirky variations can be traced back to specific beers—the McAuslan Cream Ale in Québec and the Russell Brewing cream ale in B.C. Following the success of these two beers, other brewers chose to brew similar beers and name them cream ale so that the customer could make a connection. As a result, quite confusingly, both traditional and non-traditional cream ales coexist in these two provinces. Adding to this confusion, a few British ales of varying styles are labelled "cream ale" because they are nitrogenated. This is in reference to the creamy mouthfeel that the use of mixed gas imparts.

Fun for: A late lunch

Pairs with: Light-flavoured, creamy foods, like cream of cauliflower soup

Also labeled: Present-Use Ale

Examples: Begbie Cream Ale, Mt Begbie Brewing Co., CAN; Genesee Cream Ale, USA; Kiwanda Cream Ale, Pelican Pub & Brewery, USA; Sleeman Cream Ale, CAN

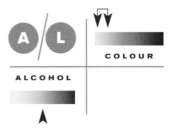

Kölsch

Kölsch is a German style from the city of Cologne (Köln in German). Usually quite pale, leaning towards straw or light gold, and crystal clear, Kölsch is dry with an understated malt character of fresh grain that, very occasionally, has a hint of sweetness.

The Kölsch-style golden ale has a more pronounced bitterness than its American-style counterparts; its finish is often described as slightly tart. The use of German hops makes for subtle, earthy aromas and flavours. There is often a hint of fruit in the nose, sometimes accompanied by a delicate sulphur or mineral note. This restrained yeast character is a result of cold-conditioning after fermentation, in a similar way to lager beers.

In Germany, the name Kölsch is a controlled appellation protected by the Kölsch-Konvention of 1985, meaning that if the beer is not from Cologne or among the breweries included in the Konvention, it cannot be given the name Kölsch. While they are not legally bound to do so, some North American brewers choose to respect the Konvention. Others do label their beer as Kölsch as it is a clear indication of what's in the bottle.

Fun for: Outdoor summer festivals

Pairs with: Light, fresh foods, like green salad

Also labeled: Lagered Ale, Cologne Style Lager, Koln Style Beer

Examples: Arctic Ale, Swans Brewery, CAN; Kölsch, Schlafly Beers, USA; Lug-Tread Lagered Ale, Beau's All Natural Brewing Co., CAN; Sky Blue Ale, Carolina Brewery, USA; Sunbru Kölsch-Style Ale, Four Peaks Brewing Co., USA

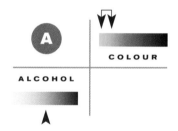

A Konvention-al Vessel

The Kölsch-Konvention covers more than Kölsch producers; it also dictates the kind of glass that is considered to be the proper serving vessel for the style. The glass in question is a narrow six-ounce (180 mL) cylindrical vessel called a *stange*. It is meant to protect the delicate aromas and flavours of the beer by prompting frequent fresh pours.

Wheat Beers

At a Glance Quite simply, these are beers in which a percentage of the barley has been replaced by wheat. There are many different styles of wheat beer in the world, but the two most common are Bavarian wheat beer and Belgian wheat beer.

Overview Wheat gives beer a silky mouthfeel, as well as a full head of foam. To the flavour, it adds a gentle bready note. Contrary to popular belief, wheat does not make beer cloudy. It is true that some wheat beers are cloudy, but that's because it is traditional not to filter them. Filtered wheat beers are just as transparent as any.

They are light and effervescent, great for warm afternoons and patio drinking. Many examples have soft fruity and spicy notes that make them an ideal accompaniment for brunch. You can even blend a wheat beer with orange or grapefruit juice to make a beer mimosa.

Wheat beers are fun to share with people who aren't sure that they like beer. The combination of gentle fruit notes, smooth silky mouthfeel and lack of bitterness in the finish might just win them over.

Belgian Wheat Beer

Belgian wheat beers are pale gold in colour and cloudy (unfiltered). The use of coriander seeds and orange peel for spicing gives them a distinct flavour and aroma. The wheat traditionally used to brew them is unmalted, resulting in a slightly tart character and a lighter colour in the finished beer.

Although Belgian breweries did adopt the use of hops in beer, most traditional Belgian beer styles have a muted hop character. In the case of Belgian wheat beer, hops take a back seat, letting the spices shine, complemented by wheat notes and often a light spicy or peppery note from the yeast. The creamy texture of Belgian wheat beers is offset by a bold carbonation and sometimes a light tartness or acidity in the finish, resulting in a beer that is quite refreshing.

This style has been around since the Middle Ages and come to us from the Flemish part of Belgium, in the area just east of Brussels. With the rising popularity of lagers in the twentieth century,

Belgian wheat beers fell out of favour, and the style might have disappeared entirely if not for the efforts of one Pierre Celis, of Hoegaarden, a town once known for producing wheat beers. He decided to revive the style in the 1960s, and founded the De Kluis brewery, producing a traditional wheat beer that he named after the town. The De Kluis brewery and Hoegaarden wheat beer were eventually acquired by Interbrew, now Anheuser-Busch InBev.

Fun for: Patio season

Pairs with: Sweet and sour foods, like mango salad

Also labeled: Wit, Witbier, Blanche, White

Examples: Allagash White, USA; Blanche de Chambly, Unibroue, CAN; Hoegaarden, BEL; White Bark Ale, Driftwood Brewing Co., CAN; ZON Belgian-Style Witbier, Boulevard Brewing Co., USA

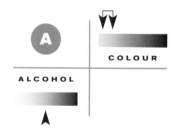

Bavarian Wheat Beer

Bavarian wheat beer is traditionally brewed with an ale yeast that gives it distinct bold, fruity and spicy notes. These are commonly described as banana and clove, although some will also find vanilla, nutmeg and lemon notes.

Like their Belgian counterparts, Bavarian wheat beers are unfiltered and golden but they tend to be a bit darker than Belgian wheat beers. The balance of aromas and flavours highlights their wheat and yeast character over hops. These beers generally have very little, if any, detectable bitterness in their finish, relying instead on a bold carbonation to lend a gentle acidity.

Interestingly, Bavarian wheat beers survived the passage of the Bavarian purity law in 1516, which originally decreed that all beers had to be brewed using only water, hops and barley malt. When Ger-many was unified, the purity law was extended to the whole country and remained firmly in place until 1987. Fortunately for wheat beer lovers, the Wittels-bach family, which ruled Bavaria and passed the purity law, made an exception for the Bavarian wheat beer they enjoyed so much. They had it brewed especially for them by one of the breweries under their jurisdiction despite the ban!

Fun for: Brunch

Pairs with: Light, egg-based foods, like omelettes

Also labeled: Weizen, Hefe-weizen, Weissbier, Weisse, German Wheat Beer

Examples: Beachcomber Summer Ale, Vancouver Island Brewing, CAN; Dry Dock Hefeweizen, USA; Hefeweizen, Yazoo Brewing Co., USA; Ur-Weisse, Ayinger Privatbrauerei, DEU; Side Launch Wheat, CAN

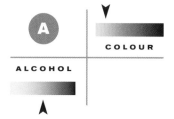

The Citrus Question

A number of bars in North America now serve Bavarian wheat beer with a slice of lemon and Belgian wheat beer with a slice of orange. This is not how these beers are traditionally served and will certainly affect how flavours are perceived. Most brewers would prefer their beer to be served as-is, feeling that fruit distracts from what they have so carefully crafted. Some breweries, however, believe fruit enhances the flavour and image of their product and encourage the practice. In the end, the choice to decorate a beer in this way is a matter of personal preference.

American-Style Wheat Beer

American-style wheat beers vary greatly in character. While they are all gold in colour, they can be filtered or unfiltered. These ales have minimal fruity character, if any, and many have a more pronounced hop character that comes through in the aroma and flavour as well as contributing some bitterness in the finish. The wheat character also varies; some examples are brewed with a detectable amount of wheat while others are simply golden ales that are brewed with a small percentage of wheat.

Kristalweizen

Traditionally, Kristalweizens are a filtered version of Bavarian-style wheat beer. In North America, however, the term is now more generally used to describe filtered wheat beers.

Berliner Weisse

See page 78.

Dunkelweizen

See page 60.

Lambic

See page 79.

Weizenbock

See page 99.

Wheat

THIS CHAPTER BRINGS TOGETHER a range of beers that all have one thing in common: they are brewed with darker malts. Dark malts get their colour from being kilned (cooked) for a longer period of time and at a higher temperature than pale malts; in some cases, they are roasted. Beer made using darker malts is easy to spot by its colour.

These malts also contribute a range of rich, earthy aromas and flavours that give a soothing, mellow quality to the finished beer whether they are the dominant note or an underlying trait. The majority of dark grains used in brewing are malted, but there are some that are not. Brewers use small quantities of unmalted grains to add specific nuances of flavour or adjust the shade of the beer slightly.

Beers brewed with these well-cooked malts have flavours that are in direct parallel with the charring on a grilled steak, the caramelization of sugars in roasted vegetables and the browning on pan-seared fish, so they are ideal companions for a range of cooked foods.

MELLOW BREWS

Amber and Dark Lagers

At a Glance Amber and dark lagers are brewed with a portion of darker malts that can take their colour as dark as black. They also add a complexity of flavour that can range from a light earthy note to intense roasted coffee.

Overview Amber and dark lagers combine the crisp, clean character of lager beer with mellow notes from darker malts. These malts are kilned or roasted more intensely, which accounts for both their colour and the aroma and flavour they contribute to beer. Dark malt notes include that of toasted-bread, bread crust, caramel, toffee, nutty, dark chocolate and coffee.

The specific malts currently used in traditional European-style dark lagers were developed in the early 1800s, as a result of newly designed equipment that cooked malts using indirect heat, allowing for greater temperature control. The heating of grains with these new kilns triggered a chemical reaction called the Maillard reaction, which browns the malts and produces rich, slightly sweet bread-crust notes. Two brewers, who were friends at the time, simultaneously introduced indirectly-fired kilns at their respective breweries, resulting in separate but distinct malts named after their respective cities of origin: Vienna malt and Munich malt.

Amber and dark lagers are great beers for those who generally enjoy golden lagers and are curious to try something different. The earthy, toasted notes in these beers will particularly appeal to those who enjoy eating root vegetables, legumes and nuts.

Märzen

Märzens have a straightforward lager profile that draws attention to their malt and hop character. The balance of aromas and flavours in a Märzen-style beer definitely leans towards the malt, with characteristic toasted and bread-crust notes.

The Märzen style ranges in colour from a deep gold to dark brown but is most typically amber. Historical examples were darker, while some modern European versions are gold. In Bavaria, pale Märzen beer has become a distinct style (see Oktoberfest Lager on page 36). North American breweries brew Märzens in both manners. Although there is a slight sweetness to its malt character, this beer finishes dry with a discreet bitterness in the finish. There might be a hint of earthiness in the aroma and flavour from the use of German noble hops.

Märzenbier, or "March beer," comes from the state of Bavaria, in Germany. Its roots can be traced back to the days before refrigeration, when brewing good beer in warmer months was a challenge. In 1553, quality-control legislation was passed in Bavaria prohibiting the brewing of beer between St. George's Day, in April, and St. Michael's Day, in September. Brewers therefore had to create stockpiles in March. Märzen beers are brewed to be slightly higher in alcohol, generally between 5 and 6% ABV. Alcohol traditionally helped them keep through the summer, although the style is now brewed year-round.

Fun for: Fall celebrations

Pairs with: Grilled white meat, like turkey dinner

Also labeled: Märzenbier, Wiesn Märzen, Oktoberfest Märzen

Examples: Märzen, Gordon Biersch Brewing Co., USA; Märzenbier, Nickel Brook Brewery, CAN; Munster Fest, Three Floyds Brewing Co., USA; Red Hammer, Paddock Wood Brewing Co., CAN; Samuel Adams Oktoberfest, USA

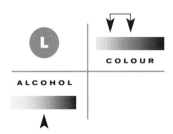

Munich Dunkel

"Dunkel" means "dark" in German. This style of lager is generally deep brown in colour, and has soft, toasted-malt tones, often complemented by richer coffee and toffee notes from the use of darker malts.

As with Märzens, malt tones dominate the aroma and flavour of Munich Dunkels, with earthy notes and bitterness from German noble hops taking the backseat. Some Dunkels have a soft sweetness to them, while others are quite dry.

The Munich Dunkel is a very old style and pre-dates the invention of indirect-fire kilning, which now allows brewers to consistently produce golden and amber beers. While modern Munich Dunkels are brewed with a good portion of Munich malts, many brewers will add a range of darker malts in order to bring the beer's colour, aroma and flavour closer to what it might have been in the early days of the style, when malts were cooked over direct fire.

Fun for: Historical re-enactments

Pairs with: Delicate spicy foods, like blackened catfish

Also labeled: Dunkel, Premium Dunkel, Münchner Dunkel, Dark Munich-Style Lager

Examples: Altbairisch Dunkel, Ayinger Privatbrauerei, DEU; Dark Cloud, Mother Earth Brewing, USA; Dark Lager, King Brewery, CAN; Hermann's Dark Lager, Vancouver Island Brewing, CAN; Penn Dark, Pennsylvania Brewing Co., USA

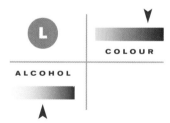

Red or Dark American Lager

These lagers are generally subtler in aroma and flavour than their European counterparts. While they do have a deeper colour, their aroma and flavour can range from being quite similar to that of a golden lager, to displaying light earthy, toasted or caramel notes and even, on occasion, hints of dark chocolate and coffee. These darker American lagers are generally sweeter than golden lagers but remain crisp and have an equally bold carbonation level.

Vienna Lager

Quite similar in style to Märzens, these lagers are generally more consistent in colour, usually pale to deep amber. Vienna lagers also have a different balance of aromas and flavours, with a softer malt profile as well as a more present hop character that includes a moderate bitterness and earthy notes. The malt character in Vienna lagers comes from the use of Vienna malts, which are cooked in a similar fashion to Munich malts, resulting in toasted-bread and, on occasion, delicate toffee notes.

Schwarzbier

Schwarzbier, or "black beer," is the darkest of the German lager styles. In addition to the sweet toasted notes of Munich malts, Schwarzbiers also have deeper coffee or dark chocolate notes that come from the use of roasted malts. It is these same malts that give Schwarzbier its black-brown colour. The bitter roasted-coffee notes in Schwarzbier will linger into the finish, on occasion accompanied by a hint of hop bitterness.

Bock

At a Glance These are strong lagers with an alcohol content above 6% ABV and, depending on the kind of bock, sometimes well above 10%. Bocks combine the clean, straightforward character of a lager with the rich, full-bodied character of higher-alcohol beers that are brewed without adjuncts.

Overview The bock style comes to us from Germany, where the use of adjuncts was outlawed for hundreds of years. In order to reach the higher-alcohol level present in bocks, brewers therefore use more malt (the source of sugars that the yeast will convert into alcohol—see page 7–8). This additional malt also results in fuller body and sometimes a hint of sweetness.

Historically, bock beers were very popular in the fall and spring. More specifically they were traditionally consumed during periods of fasting (Advent and Lent), when they were used as meal replacements. The heartier quality of bock-style beers makes them ideal for these cool transitional seasons, and their earthy malt character provides a fantastic accompaniment for spring and autumn vegetables.

Traditional Bock

Traditional bocks generally have an alcohol content under 7.5% ABV and can be light to dark brown. This deeper colour comes from the use of darker malts that also provide rich toasted-bread notes.

Traditional bocks have a medium body and their higher alcohol content can provide a slight warming feeling. Light caramelized notes sometimes accompany their rich toasted-bread notes. While these lagers do have a gentle, lingering malt sweetness they are never syrupy or oversweet. The hop bitterness in traditional bocks is understated and usually just enough to balance the richer malt tones that are the dominant note in these beers.

It is generally accepted that the traditional bock style originated in a town called Einbeck, which, in the late Middle Ages, was widely known for its strong beers. Many theorize that the term *bock* was derived from the city's name, because in German ordering "ein Bock" sounds very much like the name of the beer's city of origin.

Fun for: Cool spring days

Pairs with: Pork in many forms, like sausages

Also labeled: Bock, Dunkler Bock, Dunkles Bock

Examples: Anchor Bock Beer, USA; Spring Bock, Amsterdam Brewery, CAN; The Big Bock, Hoyne Brewing Co., CAN; urBock, Creemore Springs Brewery Ltd., CAN; Winter Bock, Silver City Brewery, USA

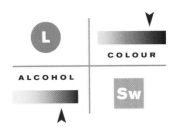

Bavarian Purity Law

The Bavarian Purity Law, or *Reinheitsgebot* in German was passed in 1516 and restricted the number of ingredients that could be used to brew beer. The original law included only water, malted barley and hops. Later on, when yeast was discovered, it was added to the list. The *Reinheitsgebot* was extended to all of Germany during unification. Owing to concerns about "free movement of goods" in the initial stages of the formation of the European Union, the law was significantly abated in 1987. The term *Reinheitsgebot* is still popular in the international brewing community with the majority of German brewers continuing to abide by it and brewers elsewhere choosing to adopt it. Unfortunately, the use of the term *Reinheitsgebot* is not regulated, leaving it open to abuse.

Doppelbock

Doppelbock means "double bock." These lagers are characterized by a higher alcohol content, which can traditionally be as high as 10% ABV and sometimes higher. Along with the additional alcohol comes a fuller body and a more pronounced warming quality.

Doppelbocks have a broader colour range than traditional Bocks, from rich gold to deep brown. Paler Doppelbocks have a combination of pale and toasted malts that imparts a sweet bready character, while darker versions use a higher proportion of toasted malts as well as darker malts, resulting in a more intense bread-crust character and, on occasion, underlying toffee and dark chocolate notes. In both cases, these malt notes are accompanied by subtle dried-fruit notes as well as pronounced alcohol notes.

The Doppelbock style was inspired by a strong bock beer brewed by monks in Munich for consumption during Lent. They called this strong lager Salvator and started selling it to the public during the 1700s. The name "Salvator" was trademarked by the Paulaner brewery when new owners took over the original recipe from the monks. As a tribute to this popular brew, many breweries choose names ending in *-ator* for their Doppelbocks.

Fun for: Tempering periods of fasting
Pairs with: Root vegetable dishes, like roasted parsnips
Also labeled: Strong Bock, Double Bock
Examples: Butt Head Bock, Tommyknocker Brewery, USA; Cameron's Deviator Doppelbock, CAN; Captivator DoppelBock, Tree Brewing Co., CAN; Paulaner Salvator, DEU; Troegenator Double Bock, Tröegs Brewery, USA

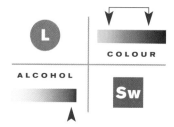

Heller Bock

Hell is the German word for "light" or "pale." Heller bocks are similar in strength to the traditional bock but lighter in colour. Consequently, they have a more delicate malt character with fresh bread-crumb notes and hints of toasted notes. Heller Bocks will often have more hop character than their darker counterparts; German hops impart earthy flavours and aromas as well as a more pronounced bitterness in the finish.

Also labeled: Helles Bock, Maibock

Eisbock

This is the strongest of the bock-style beers, with an alcohol content that is usually above 9% ABV. The name Eisbock translates to "ice bock"; in order to achieve a higher alcohol content, Eisbocks are freeze-distilled. Once they've been brewed, these beers are frozen, and ice (frozen water) is then removed, thereby concentrating the beer. Eisbocks have a rich, full body and an intense but pleasant alcohol warmth and are usually dark brown in colour. Their aroma and flavour is equally intense and these beers can be seen as a concentrated version of the Doppelbock style.

Also labeled: Ice Bock

Weizenbock

See page 99.

Amber and Dark Ales

At a Glance Amber and dark ales make up a family that combines the rich flavours of darker malts with the slightly fuller body, fruit notes and added complexity that come with the use of ale yeast.

Overview While the dark malt character in amber and dark ales can include the bread-crust notes that are characteristic of European dark lagers, it more commonly has biscuit, caramel, nutty, chocolate or coffee notes that come from British specialty malts. Although they are quite flavourful and complex, amber and dark ales are conceived for session drinking. They often have an alcohol content of 5% ABV or lower and their flavours tend to be carefully balanced so that no individual element is distracting to the drinker.

Amber and dark ales will appeal to those who generally gravitate towards more flavourful foods. In addition, the caramelized and roasted notes in these beers makes them a great accompaniment to roasted or grilled foods.

California Common

California commons are crisp, amber-coloured beers. Their flavour profile is balanced and understated, combining delicate caramel malt and fruit notes with a subtle woodsy note from hops, which also add a moderate level of bitterness.

The California common beer style is quirky; for judging purposes, it is often categorized as a hybrid style, while brewers will usually classify it as a lager. This is because this beer is brewed using a lager yeast strain, but fermented at a higher temperature. At these temperatures, despite belonging to the lager family, California common yeast strains will produce delicate pear-like fruit esters that are more commonly associated with ales.

The California common style is based on what's known as steam beer, which emerged on the West Coast of the U.S. around the time that lager yeasts were popularized in North America. Because lager yeasts ferment at lower temperatures, brewers who didn't have access to refrigeration had to find alternate ways to keep them cool. In this case, brewers used shallow open containers for fermentation, allowing the heat to dissipate. This technique resulted in fermentation temperatures low enough for certain strains of lager yeast to thrive. Modern California common beers are based on Anchor Steam Beer, which is brewed in San Francisco and was inspired by the historical steam beers of the region. Many brewers choose to use the same Northern Brewer hop variety in their California common as Anchor Brewing uses in its steam beer. It is this hop that gives the style its distinctive evergreen, almost minty hop character.

Fun for: Oceanside patios
Pairs with: Lighter foods that combine many ingredients, like pizza
Also labeled: Steam Beer
Examples: Anchor Steam Beer, USA; Cali Common, Lucky Hand Beer, USA; Dorothy's New World Lager, Toppling Goliath Brewing Co., USA; Rocket Bike American Lager, Moab Brewery, USA

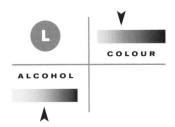

Irish Red Ale

These ales are deep reddish-amber or reddish-brown, with a rich malt profile that combines sweet toffee or caramel notes with a hint of coffee. While these malt flavours are the dominant note in Irish red ales, they can be accompanied by subtle underlying fruit notes and, on occasion, a hint of butterscotch from the yeast.

The coffee character in Irish red ales comes from the use of roasted barley. Like roasted coffee beans, these grains will contribute a distinct, dry coffee-like bitterness to the finish of these beers. This roast bitterness is sometimes supported by a delicate hop bitterness and earthy hop notes.

The term *Irish red ale* is not traditional and was never in use in Ireland. It was coined when Irish-style ruby-coloured ales were popularized in North America in the late twentieth century with the release of Killian's Irish Red. To further confuse matters, some traditional Irish Red Ale producers have started serving these beers on nitrogen (see page 62) and calling them cream ales, which is the name of an entirely different beer style.

Fun for: Listening to a Celtic jam at the pub
Pairs with: Rare red meat, like roast beef
Also labeled: Irish Cream Ale, Irish Ale
Examples: Big Caboose Red Ale, Fernie Brewing Co., CAN; Irish Red Ale, Garrison Brewing Co., CAN; O'Hara's Irish Red, Carlow Brewing Co., IRL; Red Trolley Ale, Karl Strauss Brewing Co., USA; Samuel Adams Irish Red, USA

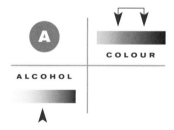

English Brown Ale

These can be pale to deep brown and the malts that give them their colour also impart rich aromas and flavours that include notes of caramel, toffee, biscuit, toast, nut, licorice and dark chocolate.

Although they share a characteristically rich malt quality, English brown ales display a range of characters. Some examples are quite dry and nutty while others have a rich toffee sweetness. Their fruity notes also vary; sometimes fresh Bosc pear or red-apple notes are present and sometimes they lean more towards dried fruits, like raisins. British ale yeasts occasionally contribute an extremely subtle butterscotch note to these beers.

The alcohol content of English brown ales ranges from around 3% to just over 5% ABV. They generally have a medium body and low carbonation and are traditionally brewed with British hops that contribute grassy, fruity or herbal notes. Some examples have a pronounced bitterness and hop character, others a lingering rich malty finish.

Fun for: Dinner at the pub
Pairs with: Beef-based North American pub foods, like hamburgers
Also labeled: Brown Ale
Examples: Black Oak Nut Brown Ale, CAN; Gahan Iron Bridge Brown Ale, Prince Edward Island Brewing Co., CAN; Old Boy, Parallel 49 Brewing Co., CAN; Red Hydrant Brown Ale, Big Dog's Brewing Co., USA; Sierra Blanca Nutbrown, USA

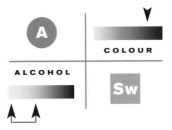

Milds

Milds, which come to us from England, are low-alcohol beers, usually under 4.5% ABV. While these ales may have a delicate grassy or fruity hop character and detectable bitterness, the balance of their flavours and aromas generally lean more towards the malt. Mild ales range from amber to brown in colour and, because their colour is a result of the malts used to brew them, their malt flavours will vary accordingly. Traditional ale yeasts will also generally add delicate fruit and sometimes a hint of butterscotch to these brews.

American Amber, Red and Brown Ales

American amber, red and brown ales combine the caramel, toffee, nut, chocolate or coffee notes of darker malts with the bold character of West Coast U.S. hop varieties. These hops contribute a distinct bitterness in the finish of the beer as well as lively aromas and flavours that might include citrus notes, tropical fruit notes or resinous notes. As a general rule, American amber ales will have a more pronounced hop character than their darker counterparts, but there are exceptions.

Scottish Ale

Scottish ales tend to be low-alcohol, generally under 5% ABV and sometimes as low as 2.5%. These amber-to-brown-coloured beers are traditionally categorized by intensity, with a nod to the varying cost, in shillings, of barrels of beer in Scotland in the nineteenth century. Their malt tones usually have a distinct caramelized note that can sometimes be accentuated by a delicate butterscotch note from the yeast. This malty sweetness is followed by a dry finish, punctuated by a detectable hop bitterness. Some modern interpretations include a hint of peat that comes from the use of the peat-smoked malts commonly associated with Islay scotches, but this is not traditional to the style (see page 98).

Also labeled: 60/-, 70/-, 80/- (sixty-, seventy- and eighty-shilling). These three subcategories of Scottish ale are alternately known as light, heavy and export Scottish ales.

Dunkelweizen

This is a darker version of Bavarian wheat beer (see page 43) brewed with the addition of darker European malts. It has richer toasted notes as well as a darker colour, but retains the traditional yeast characteristics of banana and clove.

Scotch Ale

See page 98.

Porters and Stouts

At a Glance Porters and stouts are ales brewed with a percentage of roasted barley. Roasted grains give these beers a dark colour that ranges from a deep brown to an intense, opaque black as well as rich dark chocolate and coffee notes.

Overview While the various styles of porters and stouts range in character, they share similar traits, having all evolved from the porter style of beer, whose reputation spread throughout Europe in the 1700s. Porters and stouts are often thought of as being heavy and intense. This is partly because of their appearance, especially in the case of opaque pitch-black examples. The roasted flavours in these beers can initially seem overwhelming to those who do not generally enjoy bitter foods.

Coffee drinkers and lovers of dark chocolate, however, will often gravitate to these beer styles in which they will find familiar flavours. Like coffee and chocolate, porters and stouts can be comforting on grey, dreary days.

Stouts

Stouts are dark brown or black, and opaque. Their dominant note is often described as coffee or dark chocolate. The roasted grains that provide these aromas and flavours also add a dry bitter finish to the beer and, on occasion, a hint of coffee-like acidity.

Stouts are British ales; in addition to a roasted character, they can present a touch of fruitiness or butterscotch from the yeast. They might have a hint of grassy or fruity British hop aroma and flavour but the hop bitterness is fairly low, generally allowing the coffee-like bitterness of the roasted grains to stand out and linger into the finish.

There are sub-styles of stout (see page 65), which will often include a specific style name on their label. Beers labelled simply as "stout" are likely in the range of 4–6% ABV with a dominant coffee-like roast character in their finish that can verge on tasting burnt. Their carbonation levels tend to be low (see sidebar). These beers can be quite dry, with a finish that almost seems sour. Some stouts are brewed with the addition of oats, which give them a slightly fuller body and creamy texture. Oats also add a delicate nutty aroma and flavour. Oatmeal stouts are not generally sweet, but some brewers choose to add caramelized malts, resulting in a semisweet-chocolate note.

Fun for: A rainy day

Pairs with: Salty foods. Oysters are a classic pairing

Also labeled: Irish Stout, Dry Stout, Oatmeal Stout

Examples: Back Road Stout, Millstream Brewing Co., USA; Diamond Head Oatmeal Stout, Howe Sound Brewing Co., CAN; Guinness, IRL; St. Ambroise Oatmeal Stout, McAuslan Brewing Co., CAN; Stagecoach Stout, Figueroa Mountain Brewing Co., USA

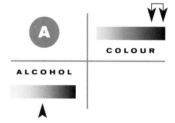

Tiny Bubbles

In the 1950s, Guinness developed a dispensation technique that involved blending nitrogen with carbon dioxide both in the beer and for serving it. This gas blend, combined with custom spouts that restrict the flow of beer through the faucet, are responsible for the tiny bubbles, cascading effect and dense foam often associated with stout. Because nitrogen is not as soluble in beer, the result is a much lower carbonation level than in a beer made and served with pure carbon dioxide. The lower level of CO_2 also results in a mellower flavour, since carbon dioxide adds an acidic bite.

Porter

Porters are light to dark brown in colour. Like stouts, they have roasted notes but these tend to be mellower, with a dark chocolate or cocoa character. Some porters will have a hint of coffee but their finish usually won't have the same intensely roasted character as that of stouts.

Like stouts, porters are ales and can have subtle underlying fruit and butterscotch notes. Porters will generally have a more elaborate malt character, however, that includes caramel, toffee and nutty notes and, on occasion, a hint of smoke. Their overall malt profile can be dry or semisweet and is generally balanced by a detectable hop bitterness.

The porter style was born in London in the early 1700s. It was extremely popular and soon spawned a bolder version known as the stout porter (the term *stout*, at the time, was used to designate a bolder version of any beer style). As time wore on, the term was shortened to stout. By the late 1800s, the original porter style had taken a few turns before falling out of favour and gradually disappeared before being revived by the craft beer movement in the late twentieth century. Most porters are in the 4–5.5% ABV alcohol range and will have earthy, grassy or fruity notes from the use of British hops. Robust versions will be very dark, a bit stronger in alcohol—up to 6.5%—and might make use of bolder American hop varieties.

Fun for: Celebrating the end of a long day of work

Pairs with: Hearty traditional pub food, like steak-and-kidney pie

Examples: Black Death Porter, Russell Brewing Co., CAN; La Gaspésienne no.13, Microbrasserie Pit Caribou, CAN; Peter Brown Tribute Ale, Bear Republic Brewing Co., USA; Pluff Mud Porter, Holy City Brewing, USA; Porter, Founders Brewing Co., USA

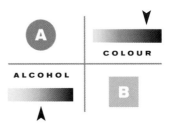

Baltic Porter

Baltic porters are generally deep reddish-brown to black-brown in colour and higher in alcohol, with an ABV over 7% and sometimes as high as 10%. As a result, these porters have a full body and soft alcoholic warmth.

The malt character in Baltic porters includes dark chocolate notes and sometimes a hint of smoke from roasted grains. There is often an underlying sweetness that takes on a caramelized, toffee, dark sugar, molasses or licorice flavour. Baltic porters also have a dark-fruit complexity that is reminiscent of fortified wine and often includes plum, black cherry or raisin notes. They will sometimes have a hint of spicy or earthy hop aromas and flavours and their finish combines hop bitterness with a rich, lingering dark chocolate note.

Baltic porters are generally lagers. This beer style developed in the Baltic states in the 1700s, when porter-style beers were all the rage, and was likely influenced by the Russian imperial stouts (see page 96) that were being brewed in England and shipped to Russia, presumably through Baltic ports. Although these strong beers would probably originally have been brewed as ales, as the popularity of lager brewing swept across Europe, Baltic porters evolved into lagers resulting in the clean, strong, dark lager beers we know as Baltic porters today.

Fun for: Outdoor winter festivals
Pairs with: Confections from caramelized sugar, like toffee
Examples: Baltic Porter, Uncommon Brewers, USA; Baltic Porter de l'ancrier, Hopfenstark, CAN; Baltic Thunder Baltic Porter, Victory Brewing Co., USA; Grand Baltic Porter, Garrison Brewing Co., CAN

American Stout

These stouts are bolder in aroma and flavour than their European counterparts and have a higher alcohol content, although not as high as the Russian imperial stout. They have trademark roasted dark chocolate and coffee notes that can include a hint of smoke. Accompanying these notes are distinct fruity or resinous aromas and flavours and a bold bitterness that all come from the use of American hops.

Milk Stout

Milk stouts range in alcohol from 3 to 6% ABV. They come to us from England and are brewed with the addition of lactose, a type of sugar commonly found in milk. Lactose gives these beers a fuller body than other stouts in the same alcohol range and contributes an underlying sweetness that, depending on the beer, can range from being quite subtle to moderately sweet. In sweeter examples, the combination of lactose and roasted notes result in a flavour profile that is reminiscent of coffee and cream.

Also labeled: Sweet Stout, Cream Stout

Russian Imperial Stout

See page 96.

THIS CHAPTER COVERS A WIDE
range of beers whose ingredients impart vibrant, distinct flavours. Pale ales and India pale ales share a conspicuous, hop-derived bitterness. The beers in the sour ales category, meanwhile, are fermented with the assistance of bacteria, which give them a zesty acidity. Fruit ales and spiced ales range greatly in personality, but share a tendency to surprise and amuse.

Though some people are instantly drawn to the complexity and exuberance of these beers, notes of bitterness and acidity can be an acquired taste. Skeptics and doubters who take the time to familiarize themselves with these brews, however, tend not to regret it. Many beer drinkers whose initial reaction to a bitter, hoppy brew was to flinch have wound up as aficionados—or "hop heads," as they're known in the beer world.

The beers in this chapter are well suited for small, everyday celebrations and lively occasions. Their spirited flavours, meanwhile, pair well with a wide range of bold, complex foods.

Pale Ales

At a Glance Pale ales range from gold to copper. Their flavour carefully balances soft bread, biscuit, toast or caramel notes from malt with a pronounced hop flavour and bitterness.

Overview Pale ales are not, by modern standards, particularly pale in colour. The name dates back to a time—the late 1600s—when industrial malting technology was in its infancy and amber beer was distinctly lighter than the other beers on the market.

Like amber and dark ales, pale ales are designed for session drinking and ride the line between being full-flavoured and highly drinkable. Pale ales reward the drinker who chooses to stop and savour, but are sufficiently understated not to distract anyone who just wants to enjoy a few consecutive pints.

Their nuanced character has made pale ales hugely popular as an everyday beer, if not quite as popular as golden lagers.

English Pale Ale

English pale ales tend to be lower in alcohol, usually in the range of 3 to 5.5% ABV. Their malt profile often includes a hint of caramel, with English hops contributing grassy, herbal or floral notes along with a pronounced bitterness.

Some have a soft sweetness accompanied by a biscuit note while others have a more pronounced caramel flavour. In either case, the finish is generally dry, owing to the use of hard water. Body varies but is usually on the lighter side, as is the level of carbonation. British ale yeast imparts a delicate hint of pear or red apple or, on occasion, butterscotch.

In competitions, English pale ale is frequently divided into categories that include bitter, best bitter and extra special bitter. While these sub-styles are marked by nuances in colour, balance, body and strength, the beers they describe are basically quite similar. While all of these terms are in common use, their history is murky and many knowledgeable people feel the nomenclature is somewhat interchangeable. As a general rule, however, each of the three subcategories listed above is slightly higher in alcohol content and intensity than the previous one.

Fun for: Lunch at the pub

Pairs with: Lighter-flavoured traditional pub foods, like chicken potpie

Also labeled: Bitter, Standard Ordinary Bitter (SOB), Best Bitter, Premium Bitter, Extra Special Bitter (ESB), Special Pale Ale (SPA)

Examples: Best Bitter, Picaroons Traditional Ales, CAN; DBA, Firestone Walker Brewing Co., USA; Red Racer ESB, Central City Brewing, CAN; St. Ambroise Pale Ale, McAuslan Brewing Co., CAN; Summit Extra Pale Ale, USA

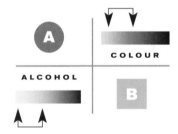

Cask-Conditioned Ales

The pale ale family of beers, and British session beers in general, are best enjoyed in cask-conditioned form. Cask-conditioned ales are easy to identify at the bar: they are served either directly from a keg-like container sitting on the bar, or by way of a hand pump rather than a regular draught faucet. Unlike kegged beers, they are not filtered or force-carbonated before being packaged. Instead, cask-conditioned beer is transferred directly into the cask in the final stages of fermentation and carbonation is brought about naturally by the still-active yeast. These old-school ales are delicious but delicate, and it takes trained and conscientious staff to store and serve them correctly.

American Pale Ale

American pale ales are gold to deep amber and generally close to 5% ABV. They tend to have a more intense flavour than English pale ales thanks to being brewed with characterful American hop varieties (see page 5).

While American pale ales can have a noticeable caramel sweetness, they are often drier than their English counterparts and more bitter in the finish. The level of yeast-derived fruitiness varies, too, with some brewers choosing to dial it up in the traditional British way and others restraining those notes to let the hop character shine.

The American hop varieties that give these pale ales and many other modern American beer styles their trademark character were developed on the west coast of the U.S. These hops, which first came onto the market in the 1970s, are known for their bitterness and bold notes, most typically of citrus, resin or tropical fruit.

Fun for: Starting the evening

Pairs with: Tex-Mex-style foods, like fajitas

Also labeled: APA, Pale Ale

Examples: Canuck Pale Ale, Great Lakes Brewery, CAN; Old Jalopy Pale Ale, Powell Street Craft Brewery, CAN; Pale 31, Firestone Walker Brewing Co., USA; Sierra Nevada Pale Ale, USA; YellowBelly Pale Ale, CAN

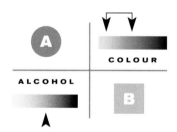

Belgian Pale Ale

Belgian pale ales are amber, with an alcohol content of around 5% ABV, and a less-pronounced hop bitterness than their English and American counterparts. They also have a bolder yeast character that often includes spicy pepper notes as well as orange or lemon-like citrus fruit notes.

The malt tones in Belgian pale ales will on occasion have a light caramel sweetness, but they often stray more towards toasted or biscuit flavours. These beers are traditionally brewed with Continental hop varieties, resulting in earthy and spicy notes as well as a gentle bitterness in the finish. Because their hop character is understated, Belgian pale ales can seem slightly sweeter than other pale ales.

Belgian brewers created this distinct beer style in the early 1900s to compete with the increasingly popular session beers then being imported.

Note: Some North American breweries choose to make American-style pale ales using characterful Belgian yeast strains and label them as Belgian pale ales. These beers are entirely different from the ones described above; they are essentially American pale ales with a spicy, peppery or earthy Belgian twist.

Fun for: Having with appetizers
Pairs with: Belgian-inspired snacks, like fries and mayo
Also labeled: Spéciale Belge
Examples: Brugse Zot, Huisbrouwerij De Halve Maan, BEL; De Koninck, BEL; Palm Speciale, BEL

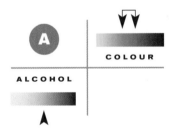

India Pale Ales

At a Glance More commonly known as IPAs, these are essentially bolder versions of pale ales with an alcohol content above 5% ABV as well as a more vibrant hop character and bitterness.

Overview India pale ales are often described as being hop-forward, with a complex aroma that can bring to mind such terms as *herbal, grassy, floral, citrus, resin, berries* and *tropical fruit.*

These are bold beers. Their bitterness can be startling to some, while others find it enthralling. Craft-brewed IPAs have really captured the public's imagination in the past ten to fifteen years. They have become one of the most popular craft beer styles in North America, with a number of breweries choosing to release multiple interpretations. IPAs are so popular that—as mentioned earlier—there's now a term to describe their fans: *hop heads.*

IPAs have an exuberant aroma and flavour. These are great beers to enjoy on lively occasions. Their zesty hop character will appeal to those who enjoy eating grapefruit and bitter greens.

English IPA

Amber- to copper-coloured with an alcohol content that can climb up to 7.5% ABV, these beers have a bold character that expresses the herbal, fruity and grassy notes typical of English hops.

English IPAs are hop-forward, but their bitterness is balanced by a host of other flavours. These beers are generally medium-bodied with slightly sweet notes of bread, biscuit or caramel from the malt. Their complex character can also include pronounced pear or apple notes sometimes accompanied by a vague hint of butterscotch from the yeast as well as, on occasion, a touch of sulphur.

The name IPA has its roots in the eighteenth century and the export of British beer to employees of the East India Company. The origins of this style are surrounded in myths. One says that because beers were going bad en route to India, brewers eventually created this highly hopped, high-alcohol style to better survive the journey. Another story has it that IPA only became known in the U.K. because a ship on its way to India was wrecked and its cargo (including IPA beer) auctioned off in Liverpool.

While we can be sure that these stories are not true, it's still not known exactly how and when the IPA became its own style. We do know that many kinds of beer were successfully being exported during this time and some brewers favoured higher-alcohol, well-hopped pale ales knowing that they kept better in warmer climates—hops and alcohol being natural preservatives. Still, it seems that brewers who were exporting pale ales to warm countries gradually made small changes to those beers because, by the early 1800s, India pale ale had emerged as a style of beer that was distinct from the pale ale.

Fun for: After a visit to the museum
Pairs with: Rich sweet and spicy dishes, like curry
Also labeled: IPA, British IPA
Examples: Brooklyn East India Pale Ale, USA; India Pale Ale, Goose Island Beer Co., USA; IPA Anglaise, Brasserie Dunham, CAN; Russell IP'eh!, Russell Brewing Co., CAN; Silverspot IPA, Pelican Pub & Brewery, USA

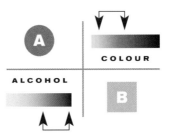

American IPA

American IPAs tend towards the lighter side of the gold-to-copper spectrum. Their dominant note is the vibrant character of West Coast American hops.

Like their English counterparts, American IPAs can have an alcohol content as high as 7.5% ABV. They generally have a medium body and soft caramel malt character but are often brewed to be drier and crisper than English IPAs. As with American pale ales, these IPAs range in sweetness and yeast-derived fruitiness, with some examples resembling English IPAs in their balance and others allowing the hops to dominate.

Because the American IPA is such a popular style, and comes in so many versions, brewers often look for a way to differentiate their IPA from the others on the market. Some breweries devise new equipment to better infuse hops aromas and fla-vours, like Sierra Nevada's "hop torpedo" and the Dogfish Head "Sir Hops Alot." Others brew sub-styles, like Smash, an acronym for Single (type of) Malt And Single (variety of) Hops. A number of breweries bring out these Smash beers in series, each highlighting a different hop variety.

Fun for: A summer barbecue

Pairs with: Southern U.S. cuisine, like fried chicken

Also labeled: IPA

Examples: Head Hunter India Pale Ale, Fat Heads Brewery & Saloon, USA; La Morsure, Micro-brasserie Le Trou du Diable, CAN; Little Scrapper IPA, Half Pints Brewing Co., CAN; Stone IPA, USA; Tap It Brewing IPA, USA

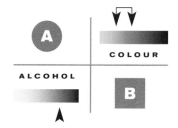

What's Floating Around in My IPA?

Many IPAs are cloudy and some even have little particles floating in them. These beers are either dry-hopped or unfiltered and sometimes both. Filtering strips out flavours and aromas, so some brewers choose to filter their IPAs roughly or not at all in order to maximize hop character.

Double IPA

These are stronger versions of American IPAs. Their alcohol content can soar up to above 10% ABV, and their aromas and flavours are dialled up accordingly. These ales have a bold hop aroma, flavour and bitterness that linger in the finish.

The alcohol in double IPAs comes through in their aroma and flavour. In addition to this, double IPAs with an alcohol content in the higher range for the style will have a warming effect. These alcohol aromas and flavours are sometimes fused with fruity-ale notes. Double IPAs can be full-bodied, but the current trend is to brew them to be fairly dry with a malt character that leans more towards bready notes than caramel. These gentle malt tones are meant to be just present enough to provide balance for the bold, fresh, lively American hop character.

The double IPA style is generally attributed to American brewer Vinnie Cilurzo, who in 1994 put into production a version of his home-brewed IPA for the Blind Pig brewery of California. His recipe for Inaugural Ale doubled the quantity of hops he'd been using at home. Although Cilurzo conceded that his first batch of double IPA was bracingly bitter, "like licking the rust off a tin can," he thought it interesting enough to bring to the public. Nowadays, a number of American breweries produce a double IPA as a part of their regular beer lineup.

Fun for: Watching the sunset

Pairs with: Richer smoked meats, like barbecue ribs

Also labeled: Imperial IPA, Extreme IPA, DIPA

Examples: Endeavour, Saint Arnold Brewing Co., USA; Cafe Racer 15, Bear Republic Brewing Co., USA; Imperial IPA, Central City Brewing, CAN; Twice as Mad Tom, Muskoka Brewery, CAN; Imperial IPA, Garrison Brewing Co., CAN

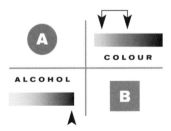

Belgian-Style IPA

This is a relatively new style combining the hop character of American IPAs with the complex spicy, peppery, earthy and fruity notes of Belgian yeast. These beers are generally amber, but some are a bit darker and their alcohol content can climb into the 9–10% ABV range. This style is brewed both by North America and Belgian breweries.

Black IPA

Black IPAs are, as their name implies, not pale at all. The creation of this relatively new, very dark-coloured style is generally attributed to the team at Vermont Brewpub, who came up with the first batch of Blackwatch IPA in 1994. Because it is relatively new, variations on this style are still being explored and parameters have yet to be clearly defined. Some black IPAs taste exactly like American IPAs and are simply darker in colour, while others taste like a cross between an American IPA and a stout.

Also labeled: India Dark Ale, India Black Ale, Cascadian Dark Ale

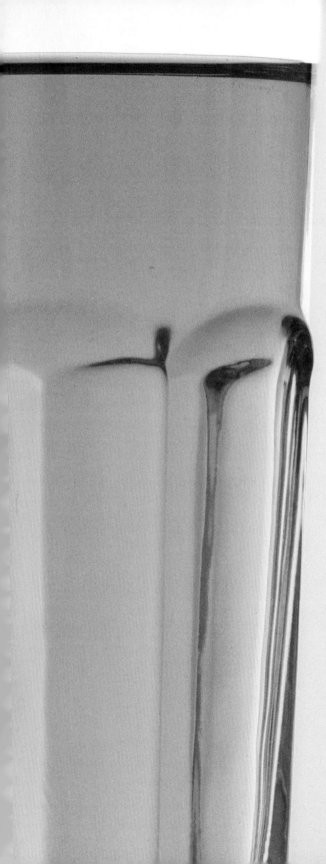

Sour Ales

At a Glance The sour note in these beers usually comes from bacteria working in tandem with yeast during fermentation to break down sugar and, in some cases, alcohol into tart-tasting compounds.

Overview Bacteria that can sour beer most commonly include various types of lactobacilli from the same family responsible for malolactic fermentation in wine. On occasion, Acetobacter, which brings about vinegar and kombucha, will also come into play.

Souring bacteria contribute a whole new dimension and added complexity to beer. The acidity they produce can either balance the richer character in intensely flavoured beers or add an incomparably tart, refreshing quality to lighter, everyday brews.

Because acidity is more commonly associated with wine, sour beers often appeal to wine aficionados. Various beers in this section have been alternately described as tasting wine-like or champagne-like.

Berliner Weisse

A combination of low alcohol content—usually below 4% ABV—light body, dry character, strong effervescence and a tart finish add up to an incredibly refreshing beer.

Berliner Weisse beers are unfiltered, and tend to be pale straw in colour and cloudy. They are brewed with a high percentage of wheat, which contributes a fresh-bread character. The yoghurt-like tartness that *Lactobacillus* bacteria give to Berliner Weisse is often accompanied by a delicate lemon or green apple-like note in the aroma and flavour.

Berliner Weisse has been brewed and served in Berlin for hundreds of years. The style likely evolved in its early years, before reaching the flavour profile we know today in the 1800s, when it was at the height of its popularity. Modern recipes take advantage of contemporary brewing technology while keeping a focus on preserving this beer's historical character. In Berlin, it is traditional to spike these sour beers with a range of sweet syrups, the most common one being a green woodruff syrup, or *Waldmeister Getränkesirup* in German.

Fun for: Hot summer days

Pairs with: Fresh fruit, like raspberries

Examples: Berlin Alexanderplatz, Hopfenstark, CAN; Hottenroth Berliner Weisse, The Bruery, USA; Professor Fritz Briem 1809 Berliner Weisse, DEU

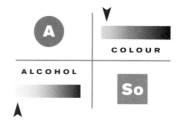

Lambic

Lambics are very dry amber-coloured beers with an alcohol content around 5% ABV. Their unusual and complex character combines a pronounced acidity with a multilayered aroma and flavour that can include rhubarb, lemon, red-apple, dusty books, cheese rinds, wet goat, wood, horse blanket and earthy notes.

Lambics are unlike any other beer style. In fact, they are the one style that is not categorized in either the lager or ale family. This is because lambics are actually spontaneously fermented by a host of different yeasts and bacteria. Another quirky thing about these beers is that their ingredients include stale hops, which contribute preservative qualities without adding bitterness.

Making lambic beer is an elaborate process and generally takes two to three years from start to finish. The "spontaneous" brewing technique dates from the days before yeast and fermentation were completely understood. It is a delicate procedure and, in order to keep noxious bacteria at bay, is only performed during the cooler months. Instead of using specific cultivated yeast cultures, lambic brewers pour the hot wort into a wide shallow vessel in a small room on the top floor of the brewery and open the windows. As the wort cools, airborne wild yeast and bacteria find their way into it and microorganisms present in the brewery are collected by steam as it condenses and drips back into the wort. From there, the inoculated wort is transferred into barrels where it ferments and conditions for years as residing organisms work in succession to give this beer its unique flavour profile. Another singular trait of lambic is that it is flat; this is because wooden barrels are porous and the beer loses carbonation as it matures.

Fun for: Sharing with friends
Pairs with: Fish soups, like waterzooi
Also labeled: Spontaneously Fermented Beer, Lambic-Style Beer
Examples: Grand Cru Bruocsella, Brasserie Cantillon, BEL

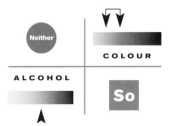

Gueuze

Gueuze beers are a blend of aged lambic with younger lambic that has only spent six to twelve months in barrels. The older beer contributes multilayered complexity of flavour, the younger a lively carbonation.

Gueuze beers can involve blending a number of batches of lambic to achieve a desired flavour. This artful process is sometimes done at the brewery, but there are also specialized blending houses that source their lambic elsewhere. The resulting beer is packaged in corked bottles where, thanks to the presence of sugars and active microorganisms in the young lambic, it continues fermenting for a period of four to six months, developing a fine champagne-like effervescence.

Gueuzes generally have an alcohol content in the 5–8% ABV range. Their colour, flavour and complexity are similar to those of lambics. Their mouthfeel, however, is completely different owing to their carbonation level as well as a warming effect in those with a higher alcohol content. Many breweries choose to sweeten gueuze, which is naturally dry. In order to distinguish unsweetened examples, most lambic producers use the term *oude gueuze*, which is protected under the European Union's agricultural product quality policy and only applies if no sweetener has been added and one of the lambics used in the blend is at least three years old.

Fun for: Celebratory toasts
Pairs with: Shellfish, like steamed mussels
Also labeled: Geuze
Examples: Boon Oude Geuze Mariage Parfait, BEL; Gueuze 100% Lambic Bio, Brasserie Cantillon, BEL; Gueuze Girardin, BEL; Oude Gueuze, 3 Fonteinen, BEL; Oude Geuze, Oud Beersel, BEL

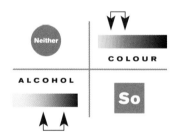

An Inimitable Flavour

The term *lambic* refers specifically to spontaneously fermented beers from the Payottenland region of Belgium and holds a Traditional Speciality Guaranteed designation, meaning it is protected under the European Union's agricultural product quality policy. This makes a lot of sense, because the bacterial fauna in different areas are quite specific and therefore result in distinct products.

Flanders Red-Brown

These ales are brown in colour, often with a reddish hue, and an alcohol content around 5–6% ABV. Because they are oak-aged and have a delicate acidity, they are often compared to red wine.

The acidity of these beers comes from a mixed fermentation and prolonged maturation. They spend between four and a half months and two years in large oak vats. During this time, a soft yoghurt-like lactic acidity develops, often accompanied by a hint of vinegar-like acetic acid. Although Flanders red-browns are generally quite dry, their malt profile will sometimes include a hint of sweetness. Malt flavours are generally toasted and accompanied by tannic notes from the oak as well as cherry, red currant and red wine notes. There is no detectable bitterness in the finish, which tends to be dry with a crisp acidity. The balance of flavours in Flanders red-brown beers is delicate and usually achieved by blending.

The practice of aging beers for a long time in order to develop a controlled acidity pre-dates the common use of hops in beer as a natural preservative. Acidity is also a preservative and protects beer from microbial spoilage, which would likely have been a common problem in the Middle Ages.

Fun for: Bringing to a dinner party

Pairs with: Simply prepared crustaceans or molluscs, like octopus salad

Also labeled: Flemish-Style Red Ale, Flanders Red Ale, Oud Bruin

Examples: Bird of Prey, Driftwood Brewing Co., CAN; Duchesse de Bourgogne, Brouwerij Verhaeghe, BEL; Oude Tart, The Bruery, USA; Petrus Oud Bruin, Brouwerij Bavik, BEL; Rodenbach Grand Cru, BEL

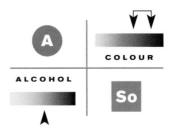

Fruit and Spiced Beer

At a Glance The beers in this chapter were brewed with the addition of fruits or spices. These ingredients can dramatically alter the character of a beer.

Overview Fruits and spices can be added to any style of beer. In addition to this, these ingredients can alter every aspect of the beer they're in, including colour, mouthfeel, aroma, flavour and finish. There is therefore a lot of variety in this chapter.

Fruits and spices are sometimes a subtle addition, providing an added nuance of flavour that will complement or accent other notes in the base beer. At other times, when added in larger quantities, they become the dominant note.

Examples with pronounced fruit or spice flavours can agreeably surprise those who aren't generally drawn to other styles of beer.

Fruit Beer

Beers brewed with the addition of fruit range vastly in character, depending on the fruit and how it was used in the brew.

Fruit beers can be either sweet or quite dry. When fresh fruits, purées or concentrates are added before fermentation, yeast consumes the majority of their sugars, resulting in a drier beer with subtle fruit notes. Some brewers prefer to add the fruit later to achieve a bolder flavour. Others use fruit syrup, which ensures more consistency in flavour from batch to batch than fresh fruit. It can also result in an artificially sweet note, depending on the quality of the syrup.

Many drinkers are under the regrettable impression that fruit beer is not really beer. To make matters worse, these beers are often marketed towards women, alienating many men (who don't know what they're missing). The notion that added fruit is a marketing gimmick is quite wrong; it's been a beer ingredient for thousands of years.

Fun for: A summer picnic

Pairs with: Custard-based dishes that aren't too sweet, like quiche

Also labeled: Kriek (cherry), Framboise (raspberry)

Examples: 4 Way Fruit Ale, Howe Sound Brewing Co., CAN; Amsterdam Framboise, CAN; Aprikat, Alley Kat Brewing Co., CAN; CoCoNut PorTeR, Maui Brewing Co., USA; Raison D'Être, Dogfish Head Brewery, USA

Spiced Beer

_____

As with fruit, herbs and spices can be added to any beer style, resulting in a wide range of flavour profiles.

_____

More traditional spiced beers might use bittering agents like dandelion, gentian root and spruce while modern interpretations can involve pretty much any herb or spice. Commercial beers have been brewed with curry and tandoori spices, myrrh and hot peppers.

Spiced beers are particularly popular in the cooler months. It is common to find pumpkin beers in the fall; while many of these beers are actually brewed with pumpkin, there are a few that simply use a pumpkin-pie spice blend and earthy malt tones to mimic pumpkin-pie flavours. Over the winter holidays, breweries often release strong beers with a festive blend of cinnamon, nutmeg, ginger and clove.

The main plant added to beer these days for flavouring is hops. In the Middle Ages, however, before hops were commonly used in beer, many other spices were used to balance the richer malt tones in beer. At that time, brewers in Europe often used a pre-blended spice mix called gruit, which was often tightly controlled and used to regulate and tax beer production.

Fun for: The winter holidays
Pairs with: Coffee cakes, like walnut cake
Also labeled: Gruit Ale
Examples: Hardywood Gingerbread Stout, USA; La Belle Saison, À l'abri de la tempête, CAN; Midnight Sun Espresso Stout, Yukon Brewing Co., CAN; Route des épices, Microbrasserie Dieu du ciel!, CAN; Utah Sage Saison, Epic Brewing Co., USA

Pour Me a Pizza

It's not only fruits and spices that can add a tasty twist to beer. Craft brewers and home brewers all over the world are having fun experimenting with unusual ingredients, often with surprisingly tasty results. Examples of kooky flavourings found in commercially available beer include coffee, salt, tobacco, lobster, graham crackers, smoked meat, marshmallows, pizza toppings, peanut butter and gummy bears.

Some spices that are used in beer.

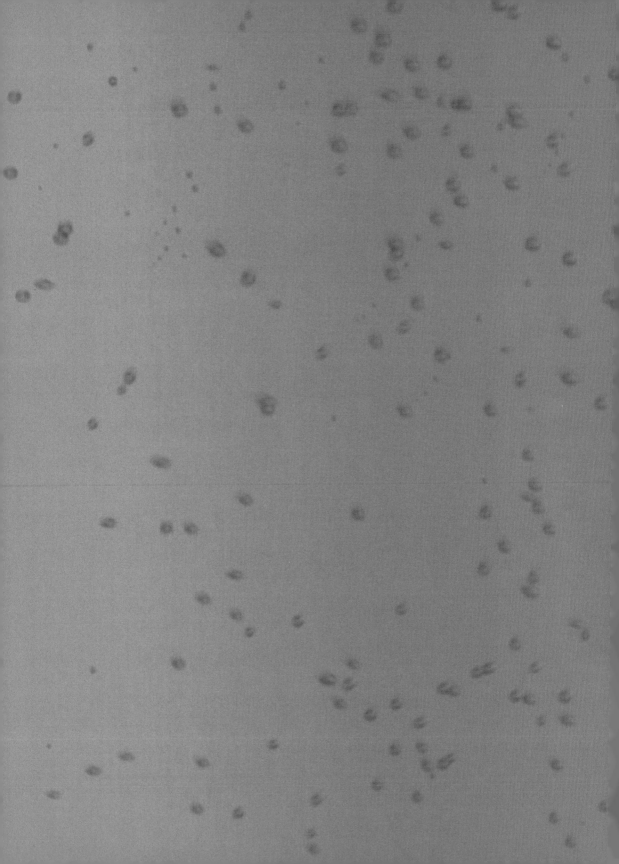

THE BEERS IN THIS CHAPTER present a complexity of notes that will reveal themselves to the drinker who slows down and pays attention.

This depth of flavour, coupled with an alcohol content that brings them into the same sphere as wine, makes these beers popular at the table. Many of the styles in this section come from Belgium, where beer is commonly consumed with meals. Some theorize that the strong ales that evolved into barley wine became popular in England in the early 1700s, at a time when it was difficult and costly to acquire wine. Strong ales were brewed and aged, at private estates, to taste as wine-like as possible and were served in lieu of wine or brandy.

The beers in this chapter also stand alone and many drinkers prefer to enjoy them without the distraction of food. They are great to linger on during tranquil, reflective, solitary moments as well as quiet gatherings with loved ones.

Captivating Brews

Farmhouse Ales

At a Glance These beers come to us from the rural areas of northern France and Wallonia in southern Belgium. Venturing into these styles requires a sense of adventure because there is so much variation and it is difficult to predict what an unknown brand will taste like.

Overview Farmhouse ales vary greatly in their character. The beers that inspired them were traditionally brewed on the farm and consumed there, rather than sold. Recipes weren't necessarily recorded and would have varied from farm to farm as well as from one year to the next.

One thing these ales have in common is that they tend towards a higher alcohol content, often in the 4.5–8.5% ABV range, and so are naturally preserved to survive the summer. Another thing they have in common is a character that seems rustic somehow. Most examples also have an understated complexity. The character of farmhouse ales strikes a delicate balance between being strong enough to have fortifying and preservative qualities and light enough to remain refreshing.

Saison

Saisons are the hoppiest Belgian beer style, and usually have a pronounced bitterness in their finish.

Dark gold or amber in colour, these ales were historically brewed on farms, at the tail end of the winter, to be gradually consumed by hardworking farmhands during the hot summer months, and likely made use of whichever grains were left in the pantry at that time. Modern commercial interpretations are therefore brewed with any of a range of grains that will add nuances of flavour.

Beyond containing an assortment of grains, it is not uncommon for saison recipes to also include herbs or spices. Again, it is likely that traditional versions would have been seasoned with whatever was handy. The ale yeasts used to brew these beers tend to be quite characterful, often contributing fruit notes that are perceived as orange or citrus, as well as spicy clove or black peppery notes. Because saisons were traditionally set aside for a period of time, modern interpretations sometimes include a soft sourness or earthy character that was once the result of aging.

Despite this complexity of flavour, saisons are brewed to be refreshing; these ales tend to be fairly light-bodied, very dry and highly carbonated.

Fun for: Bringing to a potluck dinner
Pairs with: Funky foods, like washed-rind cheeses
Also labeled: Farmhouse Ale
Examples: Bam Bière, Jolly Pumpkin Artisan Ales, USA; Carnevale, The Lost Abbey, USA; Farmhand Ale, Driftwood Brewing Co., CAN; Saison Dupont, BEL; Saison Station 55, Hopfenstark, CAN

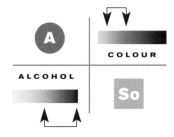

Bière de Garde

Bières de garde—"beers for keeping" or "beers that have been kept or conditioned"—are generally associated with the Nord-Pas-de-Calais region of France. They are subtler in their complexity than their Belgian counterparts and their flavour profile leans more towards the malt.

These beers range greatly in colour, from a deep gold to brown. Their malt character varies accordingly, but is generally rich without being overly sweet and includes toasted notes and, on occasion, hints of toffee or caramel. Accompanying the clean malty character of bières de garde is a delicate yet distinct note often described as cellar-like or cork-like. Hops are understated, providing little to no detectable bitterness and, at times, hints of earthiness and spice. Otherwise, the character of bières de garde is quite clean thanks to a long conditioning period. Although these beers are usually ales, some are brewed with lager yeasts. These farmhouse ales were originally aged for a long time before serving; old written accounts describe them as being wine-like and sour.

The bière de garde style faded into obscurity in the years following industrialization, but enjoyed a revival in the 1970s, when the French public became intrigued by specialty beers. Our current interpretation of the style was largely inspired by the Jenlain brand beers of Duyck brewery that rose to popularity during this revival.

Fun for: After a fall hike
Pairs with: Rich, fatty meats, like duck
Also labeled: Bière de Conserve
Examples: Biere de Mars, New Belgium Brewing, USA; Jenlain Ambrée, La Brasserie Duyck, FRA; Jenlain Blonde, La Brasserie Duyck, FRA

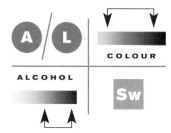

Abbey and Trappist Ales

At a Glance The styles in this category evolved from the brewing tradition developed by the Trappist order of monks over hundreds of years. The flavour profile of these ales leans more towards malt, with hop bitterness usually taking the backseat. Abbey and Trappist ales are brewed with characterful yeast strains that contribute complex fruit and spice notes.

Overview Trappist monks are a part of the order of Cisterians and follow the rule of St. Benedict, part of which dictates that they be self-sustaining. As a result, Trappist monks produce various food items both for personal consumption and to raise money for the monastery through outside sales.

Since Trappist ales are mostly defined by where they are brewed, they vary greatly in their flavour profile. One thing they do tend to have in common is a higher alcohol content, often between 6 and 11% ABV. This higher alcohol content is traditionally attained through the use of adjuncts, in the form of candi sugar that not only results in a deceptively light body, but also imparts some toffee or brown-sugar notes to the beer. Monks do brew lower-alcohol beers (see patersbier, page 94) for on-site consumption, but these are rarely available to the public.

The rich, sweet and complex fruit and spice notes in Abbey and Trappist ales, coupled with their higher alcohol content, often appeal to those with a sweet tooth, who might otherwise favour wine or cider over beer.

Dubbel

Dubbels are brown-coloured ales with an alcohol content around 6–8% ABV. They are malt-forward, with deep toast and caramelized sugar notes and sometimes a hint of chocolate.

Malt tones are accompanied by complex fruit and spice notes that often include raisin, a hint of banana, as well as pepper or clove, among others. The hop presence is discreet, and there is little if any detectable bitterness in the finish. Despite their sweeter tones, dubbels are never syrupy. They have a medium body and are often perceived as being fairly dry. Most examples are bottle-conditioned (see page 9), resulting in a carbonation that is bold but fine and feels creamy. The alcohol in these beers is usually hidden in the aroma and flavour but might come through as a slight warming sensation.

The term *dubbel* means "double," and likely dates from the Middle Ages, and the practice that monks had of brewing two beers from the same mash. The first part of the mash would be used to brew a strong beer that was reserved for guests, special occasions and outside sales. The monks would then steep the grains a second time to retrieve the residual sugars and turn the resulting, more diluted wort into an everyday beer that was lighter in alcohol. The theory is that, because the first beer was brewed using roughly twice the concentration of sugars, it was called a dubbel. These beers would have traditionally been quite varied in their flavour profiles, since each monastery had its own preferred style.

Fun for: Hearty meals
Pairs with: Meat with gamey flavours, like lamb
Also labeled: Brune, Double Abbey Ale
Examples: Brother David's Double Abbey Style Ale, Anderson Valley Brewing Co., USA; Chimay Première/Red Cap, BEL; Dominus Vobiscum Double, Microbrasserie Charlevoix, CAN; Ommegang Abbey Ale, USA; Westmalle Dubbel, BEL

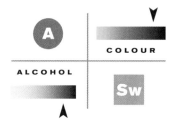

Tripel

These strong, golden-coloured ales have an ABV in the 7–10% range that gives a gentle alcohol note in the aroma and flavour as well as a warming quality. Accompanying these alcohol notes is a complex yeast character that includes banana, citrus, pepper and sometimes clove notes, among others.

Tripels are dry and medium-bodied. The vast majority of these ales are bottle-conditioned, resulting in a bold, yet smooth carbonation. Hops do play a role in the flavour profile of these beers, adding elegant floral and spicy notes to the complex aroma and flavour. The finish is long, combining a detectable bitterness from the hops with lingering alcohol and fruit notes.

This is a relatively recent style. A number of Belgian breweries, both monastic and secular, started producing golden-coloured ales in the 1920s and 1930s to compete with increasingly popular imported golden lager beers. The term *tripel* was first used commercially by the Westmalle Trappist brewery to describe a golden ale that it released in 1934. The Westmalle Tripel is widely considered to be the benchmark for the style, and the folk at Westmalle refer to it as "the mother of all tripels."

Fun for: Bringing to a cocktail party

Pairs with: Grilled oily fish, like trout

Also labeled: Trippel, Triple Belgian Beer

Examples: La Fin du Monde, Unibroue, CAN; La Tchucké, Broadway Pub, CAN; Samuel Adams New World, USA; Trippel Ale, Green Flash Brewing Co., USA; Westmalle Tripel, BEL

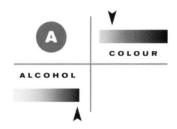

Trappist vs. Abbey

When it comes to beer, the term *Trappist* is a protected trademark, regulated by the International Trappist Association, which vets prospective members. In order to be admitted into the association and be granted permission to use the Trappist seal on their products, breweries must meet the following three criteria: the brewery must be located within the monastery walls; brewing cannot interfere with the monks' way of life and daily practice; and profits from the beer must be used either to sustain the monastery or be given to charity. Beers brewed in a way that does not meet these criteria are referred to as abbey ales. Often, these are based on a recipe that was originally developed in a monastery.

Patersbier

Patersbier translates to "father's beer." These low-alcohol beers are brewed by monks to be consumed on-site and are rarely available outside the monastery walls. Patersbiers vary greatly in style as they were traditionally brewed using the residual sugars from the mash of whichever higher-alcohol beer the monks might have been brewing.

Also labeled: Simple, Single, Enkel

Quad (Quadrupel)

The term *quadrupel* was first used commercially in 1991, by Koningshoeven Trappist brewery to describe its new amber-coloured strong ale. Since this ale was higher in alcohol than the brewery's dubbel and tripel, it seems logical to name it quadrupel. The term *quad* has since been picked up by a few North American craft breweries to describe their strong abbey-style beers.

Belgian Strong Ale

See page 99.

Strong Ales

At a Glance The beers in this category are all high in alcohol, and as a result, they have a warming quality. They are bold and fuller-bodied, often forming legs on the glass, and their mouthfeel is sometimes described as chewy.

Overview Strong ales are quite complex. Their full, rich character generally presents a soft sweetness and an elaborate interplay of aromas and flavours that often includes dried-fruit notes of raisins, prunes or figs.

The beers in this section are not designed to provide hydration and refreshment on a hot summer day. Their multilayered character is better suited to slow sipping during quiet moments in which it can better be appreciated, and their warming quality results in them being more popular during the cold months. While some examples are available year-round, a number of breweries choose to brew these ales as seasonal winter releases.

Those graced with a patient disposition will find reward in cellaring these beers and observing how their flavours evolve over time.

Russian Imperial Stout

The use of roasted grains imparts intense dark chocolate and coffee notes to the strong ales of this group and causes them to be opaquely dark brown or pitch-black.

Imperial stouts have an alcohol content in the 7–12% ABV range, and it comes through in their aroma and flavour. These ales often have a sweet caramel or molasses character, accompanied by bold dark-fruit tones that can include raisin, prune or dried cherry as well as, on occasion, delicate sweet sherry or port notes. Imperial stouts vary in their level of sweetness, but it is always balanced by a coffee-like bitterness. This note is often accompanied by a detectable hop bitterness. Traditional examples have floral, earthy or herbal hop notes and a medium bitterness, while modern American-style interpretations are characterized by a bold bitterness accompanied by the distinct aroma and flavour of American hops.

The beers that evolved into the Imperial stout that we know today were originally brewed in Britain in the late 1700s, for export to Russia, through the Baltic ports. These strong stouts were popular with the Russian court and a particular favourite of Catherine the Great, who is said to have ordered vast quantities.

Fun for: A quiet night in

Pairs with: Dark chocolate desserts, like truffles

Also labeled: Imperial Stout, Imperial Russian Stout

Examples: B.O.R.I.S. The Crusher Oatmeal Imperial Stout, Hoppin' Frog Brewery, USA; Hammer Imperial Stout, Phillips Beer, CAN; Imperial Stout, Founders Brewing Co., USA; Silver City Imperial Stout, USA; Stout Impériale, La Chouape, CAN

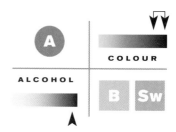

Barley Wine

Barley wines are deep gold to brown in colour and very high in alcohol, usually in the 8–12% ABV range. Their bold, full-bodied character balances a host of complex aromas and flavours.

Historically, barley wines have been defined more by their alcohol content than flavour. Although strong ales had been brewed in Britain for a while by then, it wasn't until the latter half of the 1800s that the term *barley wine* started being used to describe these beers. The Bass brewery is considered to be the first brewery to use the term on a label, in the early 1900s, to describe Bass No. 1 strong ale. From there, a number of British breweries embraced the term to describe their strongest ales.

As a general rule, barley wines are full-bodied and rich. Their flavour profile includes deep malt tones that often incorporate toast, caramel, toffee or molasses notes. These strong ales also have dried-fruit notes of raisin and prune and, on occasion, figs, as well as aromas and flavours reminiscent of forti-fied wine that are often described as sweet sherry notes. These ales can be dry or moderately sweet. The richer tones in these beers are offset by the presence of alcohol notes as well as a noticeably bitter finish. As with Imperial stouts, the hop character in these beers varies, as both traditional and modern North American interpretations exist.

Fun for: Capping off the evening

Pairs with: Intensely rich foods, like foie gras

Also labeled: Barleywine, Old Ale, Barleywine-Style Ale, Barley Wine–Style Ale

Examples: Horn Dog Barley Wine, Flying Dog Brewery, USA; Mill Street Barley Wine, CAN; Ol' Fog Burner Barley Wine, Garrison Brewing Co., CAN; Old Numbskull, AleSmith Brewing Co., USA; Thor's Hammer Barley Wine, Central City Brewing, CAN

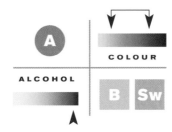

Scotch Ale

These are malt-forward beers, deep amber to brown in hue, with an alcohol content between 6 and 10% ABV. They have a distinct caramel sweetness that can, on occasion, include a hint of butterscotch.

The caramel note in Scotch ales is accompanied by an underlying complexity of flavours that includes toffee, molasses and dark chocolate malt tones as well as subtle dark-fruit notes. The hop character in these beers is restrained, providing just enough bitterness to prevent the beer from being overly sweet.

These are strong beers brewed in the Scottish tradition. They are sometimes said to be a subcategory of barley wine. Still, the way Scotch ale is interpreted today—as described above—is quite specific. In addition to this, North American craft breweries often include a hint of peat in their Scotch ales by adding some peat-smoked whisky malts.

This tendency is not traditional to Scotch ales but, rather, a modern twist. While it is true that before indirect-fire kilns came along (see page 102), malts would have contributed smoky notes to beer, this is not particular to the beers of Scotland.

Fun for: Enjoying by the fireplace
Pairs with: British game meats, like venison
Also labeled: 100, 120 or 140 Shilling Scottish Ale, Wee Heavy
Examples: Iron Duke Strong Ale, Wellington Brewery, CAN; Iron Thistle, Rahr & Sons Brewing Co., USA; Old Chub Scotch Ale, Oskar Blues Brewery, USA; Riley's Scotch Ale, Swans Brewery, CAN; Wee Heavy, AleSmith Brewing Co., USA

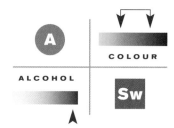

Weizenbock

Weizenbocks are a version of Dunkelweizens (see page 60) with a higher alcohol content, around 7–9% ABV. They have a fuller body and more intense flavour and aroma. Occasional examples are lighter in colour, and could be better described as a strong version of a Bavarian-style wheat beer.

Belgian Strong Ales

There is a wide range of strong ales being brewed in Belgium. These beers vary greatly in character and are notoriously difficult to categorize. For competition purposes, Belgian strong ales are often divided into three categories: Belgian golden (or pale) strong ale, Belgian dark strong ale and Belgian specialty ale, which is a catch-all category for the remaining beers.

It is difficult to make generalizations about Belgian strong ales beyond the fact that they are ales and are high in alcohol. As a general rule, though, these ales are quite complex, and often present a range of fruit and spice notes. They have a deceptively light body thanks to the use of adjuncts. Their hop bitterness is understated, allowing the malt and yeast notes to shine.

THE BEERS IN THIS CHAPTER are not united by stylistic conventions. Instead, particular ingredients or brewing techniques connect them, giving distinct notes to these beers.

The character that each of these ingredients or techniques imparts to beer is only one facet of the ultimate flavour profile. A number of brewers are investigating possibilities within each of these sections, experimenting to see how the particular dimension added by each of these ingredients and techniques will work in combination with a range of different beer styles and hybrids.

While the four categories in this chapter reflect current trends in brewing, none of them are new to the world of beer. Smoked beers, wood aging and alternative fermentation have all been a part of brewing for hundreds of years. While the current surge of gluten-free beers has certainly led to technological advances in the malting and brewing process, there are parts of the world where the traditional beers were not barley-based but instead relied on grains that grew well in those areas. For example, the *bjala* brewed in South Africa is sorghum-based, and Peruvian *chicha* is often brewed from maize.

The increasing popularity of the beers in this section reflects the current state of the North American beer industry. Now that there are a large number of well-established breweries, producers are interested in brewing beers that will stand out from the crowd and experienced brewers are looking for new personal challenges. These beers also reflect well on the North American market, as there are now a number of consumers who are adventurous in their tastes and eager to excite their taste buds with new flavour combinations.

Smoked Beer

At a Glance While there are a number of ways in which a smoky note might be introduced into beer, here, we are dealing specifically with beers that are brewed using smoked malts.

Overview Depending on the wood used as well as the percentage of smoked malt in the recipe, smoked beers can have aromas and flavours of smoke, peat, campfire, bacon or ash. In appropriate quantities and in the right beer, these notes add a pleasant complexity.

Before equipment was developed that allowed brewers to dry their malts using indirect heat, in the 1800s, all malts would likely have had a slightly smoky flavour as a result of spending some time directly over flames. This smoky note would have then transferred into the beer.

Some smoked malts are still made using direct fire, but in a more controlled fashion; others are malted and then smoked separately. The city of Bamberg and surrounding region in Germany are famous for producing smoked beer, or Rauchbier, the best-known example being Aecht Schlenkerla Rauchbier. This is one area where smoked beer has been brewed without interruption since the Middle Ages. While the region is best known for its Märzen-style smoked beers, it produces a range of beers using traditional malts that are smoked over beechwood.

More recently, brewers have started using Scottish peat-smoked malts more commonly associated with Islay scotches to spice up their Scottish-style ales. In addition, some breweries smoke their own malts using various kinds of wood chips, including alderwood, pecan, cherry, maple and juniper, to add a unique or local signature to beer.

Beer in barrels

Wood-Aged Beers

At a Glance Wood-aged beers spend some time in contact with wood, usually in the later stages of fermentation or once it is complete.

Overview Barrel aging can add all sorts of flavours to beer. Fresh barrels impart character from the wood used, oak being the most popular. Common barrel aging notes include coconut, almond, toast, clove, vanilla or leather, as well as hints of smoke, depending on the way the barrel was treated. Barrels that have previously been used for wine, spirits or cider will also transfer the character of these liquids into beer. Some barrels house microflora that will sour beer; you'll find a description of the resulting notes in the discussion of alternative fermentation that follows. Barrel aging can also affect mouthfeel, imparting dry tannic notes that are extracted from the barrel during the aging process.

Before stainless steel and keg technology came along, beers would have been fermented, conditioned and aged in either wood or clay vessels. In some areas, there are beer styles for which these traditional practices have been preserved and in which wood plays an integral role. For example, in the Flanders region of Belgium, the Rodenbach brewery ages a portion of its Flanders red-brown ales in large wooden vats that are over 150 years old.

These days, as in the wine world, some brewers choose to impart wood character to their beers through barrel aging while others will use wood chips instead. This latter technique has its advantages; it allows the brewer to use stainless-steel vessels that are already present in the brewery and are easier to sterilize. It also allows them to use types of wood unsuitable for coopering. As with the smoked beer category, brewers are now experimenting with different woods like lemon, maple, heartwood and cedar.

Alternative Fermentation

At a Glance Alternative fermentation refers to the practice of using bacteria or yeast strains beyond ale and lager yeasts (or, more precisely, yeasts that aren't in the *Saccharomyces* genus).

Overview The two most common types of bacteria used in alternative fermentation are *Lactobacillus* strains—which include pediococcus—and *Acetobacter*. Lactobacilli are known in the wine world because they are involved in the process of malolactic fermentation—they impart a soft yoghurt-like sour note to beer. Acetobacter, meanwhile, contribute a sharper vinegar-like note. They appear during the aging process and must be tightly controlled or else they will, quite literally, turn the beer into vinegar.

The most popular alternative yeast strains used in brewing beer are from the genus *Brettanomyces*,

Spontaneously fermenting beer

often referred to colloquially as "brett." These yeasts can contribute a wide range of notes to beer, including pineapple, peach, musty, barnyard horse blanket, smoke or spice, depending on the strain used. *Brettanomyces* can also ferment a wider range of sugars than ale or lager yeasts and their use generally results in an extremely dry beer.

Historically, the various organisms discussed here would have inadvertently been introduced to beer because of a poor understanding of fermentation and sanitation. Nowadays, most of the yeast strains used in brewing have been isolated and cultivated. Beer, however, had been brewed for thousands of years before yeast and fermentation were understood. Through those years, brewers triggered fermentation in various ways, transferring a portion of beer that was already fermenting into fresh wort or relying on various equipment and tools to transfer yeast from one vessel to another. Some breweries still choose to have wild yeast strains ferment their beers. A classic example is the Cantillon brewery, in Brussels. There, traditional lambic beers are brewed using yeasts that are present in the air and reside in various areas of the brewery. In addition to all of the organisms mentioned above, the fermentation of lambic beers involves a range of other *Saccharomyces* strains as well as *Tremellales* and *Enterobacters*.

Brewers now play with alternative fermentation in many ways. Some are using lambic-inspired spontaneous fermentation techniques, allowing yeast in the environment to deposit into fresh wort or encouraging flora to develop in the barrels that they use. Other brewers prefer to use a mix of cultivated strains. While most of the organisms listed in this chapter are used in conjunction with ale yeasts, some breweries are releasing beers brewed using only *Brettanomyces* strains. No matter which technique is used, alternative fermentation requires patience and vigilance in order to attain a character that is pleasant and in harmony with the other flavours present. The use of these organisms also requires strict sanitation practices to prevent them from being transferred into—and spoiling—other beers that are not meant to be sour or funky. It is also worth mentioning that, on occasion, breweries will use lactic acid as a way to achieve a sour note in their brew without introducing bacteria into the brewery.

That's Not Right

While the organisms discussed here can add a delightful complexity to beer when they are deliberately introduced and carefully controlled, poor sanitation practices can also cause them to produce unwanted notes. These unpleasant and inappropriate notes are termed "off-flavours." They sometimes develop at the brewery, but can occur at the point of service and become quite pronounced if draught systems are not being cleaned properly and regularly. Symptoms of dirty beer lines often include a combination of sour and buttery notes in the beer.

Gluten-Free Beers

At a Glance Gluten-free beers contain either a negligible amount of gluten—so small that it will not cause a reaction in those who are gluten-intolerant—or none at all.

Overview Because barley, which is the main grain used in beer, does contain gluten, a lot of gluten-free beers are brewed from other grains, most commonly sorghum, millet, rice, corn and buckwheat. The absence of barley in these beers will result in a noticeably different flavour profile, which often includes a distinct lemon-drop note.

Gluten-free beers have been on the market for a while now. Sourcing grains for them was difficult because most malting facilities are not equipped to malt a wide range of grains, which often have slightly different malting specifications than barley. The other concern, because of the specifications for gluten-free certification, was to avoid cross-contamination between gluten-free batches and barley runs. As a solution, malt companies produced a sorghum syrup that brewers could use as a base for their gluten-free beers.

Barley

In the twenty-first century, demand for gluten-free beer has increased dramatically following a growing understanding of celiac disease as well as the ensuing spike in diagnoses of gluten intolerance. As a result, the range and quality of gluten-free beers on the market is improving rapidly, with many breweries making concerted effort to produce gluten-free beers that taste as beer-like as possible. In order to achieve this, some breweries will accent other flavours and ingredients in their beers, like hops for example. Other breweries have started malting their own grains. Research is also being done into ways of removing gluten from beer that is brewed from barley.

PART THREE

Diving In

HOW TO HOST A BEER TASTING AT HOME

Hosting a beer tasting at home is a simple and delightful way to entertain, and it always makes for interesting conversation. Tasting a range of beers back to back also helps zero in on personal preferences and learn about beer. Here are a few pointers to assist in planning.

Setting Up the Space All that's really needed for a tasting is a communal area where each guest has a surface on which to put down their glasses and maybe take notes. A beer tasting is about discovering new aromas and flavours. It is therefore important to not have strong distracting odours around. Avoid cooking foods that will overwhelm the house with their aromas and ask guests to refrain from wearing scents. Even loud noises or sonic distractions such as a ringing phone can make it challenging to perceive flavour and aroma. Beyond that, it is helpful if the space is well lit so that people can better appreciate the colour of their beer and take notes comfortably, if they choose.

Eating food during the beer tasting will detract from the experience. Encourage guests to eat before coming, or serve food once the tasting is complete. If the timing of the tasting calls for food, there is always the option to throw a beer-and-food-pairing party (see page 133).

Lining Them Up The ideal number of beers for a tasting is between two and eight. Any more and the palate will be overwhelmed and the brain will tune out. To decide the order in which the beers should be served, there are a number of factors to consider. Essentially, the goal is to start with the least intense beer and work up to the most intense. This is because tasting a strong beer will make it difficult to appreciate the nuances of the one that follows. As a general rule, it's best to start with the lowest-alcohol beer first and work up to the one with the highest ABV. Having said this, it often happens that many beers in a sitting are all in the 4.5–5% ABV range. If this is the case, here are some pointers to assist in determining the serving order for those beers:

✔ Start with the lowest alcohol content, tasting the lightest beer first.

✔ A lager will generally have less intensity than an ale at the same ABV.

✔ The darker the beer, the more intense it will be.

✔ Beers with an assertive hop presence will be more intense than beers in which malt is dominant.

✔ Extremely bitter beers leave hop resins on the palate, and should only be followed by high-alcohol beers (8% ABV and over).

✔ Additional ingredients, like spices and fruits, add intensity. Place these after the malt-dominant beers but before the hop-forward ones, assuming they all have the same alcohol level.

Materials and Tools Not many supplies are needed to throw a successful beer tasting. The glasses should accommodate three to six ounces (90–180 mL), and allow room for the foam as well as some space so that guests can, if they like, swirl their beer to release aromas. The amount of each serving will depend on the total number of beers served as well as the length of the tasting. It's not ideal to have to cut a tasting short, or constantly rein things in because guests have consumed too much alcohol. Try to calculate amounts so that the total volume of beer consumed is equal to one beer an hour.

Another item that should be available during the tasting is water, which can be used as a palate cleanser between each beer. Crackers are also great to have around, again as a palate cleanser but also as a snack for guests who may not have had time to eat before arriving.

Don't Let It Sit

With beer tastings, it's not a good idea to pre-pour; as soon as a beer is opened, it starts to lose both carbonation and freshness. Taking all of the beers out of the fridge ahead of time, however, can be a good idea, especially if there is a progression of flavour intensity and alcohol content in the lineup. This is an efficient way to attain appropriate serving temperatures as the evening progresses, since the complex beers served near the end of the tasting are better appreciated at a warmer temperature than the delicate ones that will lead it.

Finally, it's always good to have paper and pens handy for those who would like to take notes. The paper provided could be a set of formal beer-tasting sheets (see pages 156–157) or simply blank sheets on which guests can jot down a few notes.

TASTING IDEAS AND GAMES Beer tastings are always enjoyable. Sampling a range of beers together as a group, sharing observations and impressions, is the most effective way to explore beer at any level. When guiding tastings, I actively encourage participation as it provides wonderful insights for everyone involved. Having the opportunity to discuss flavours while sipping along is an invaluable (and delectable) experience.

At-home tastings can be as easy and informal as sharing a selection and chatting about it. Formal ones, however, are particularly satisfying; they provide structure for the novice taster while allowing beer aficionados to focus their attention, gaining in-depth insights into one particular aspect of beer appreciation. Here are a few formats and games that can be enjoyed by a group of any size.

Beer Flavour Identification Tasting Game Beer can have myriad flavours and aromas. The beer flavour wheel (see page 158) includes more than eighty distinct flavours and aromas, and there are many more. This tasting is about picking out individual flavours in beer and putting names to them. For beginners, it might be a good idea to print out a few copies of the flavour wheel and have them handy as a guide. The Beerology beer-tasting sheet (see pages 156–157) is another great tool to use.

For this tasting, you will need a sheet of paper for each participant. This beer tasting is done one beer at a time. Pour a sample for each person and ask everyone to take a moment to taste the beer and identify three to five distinct flavours and aromas in the beer (depending on how challenging you would like the tasting to be). Once everyone is done, compare notes and look for overlap.

This tasting can be presented as a competition, awarding points for every descriptor where there is overlap. For example, if two people identify the same flavour, they each get two points. If three people identify the same flavour, they each get three points, and so on. Should two people come up with the exact same set of flavours, they can get fifty points each. With a larger group of people, this can game can also be played in teams.

Beer Description Guessing Game Describing a beer can seem challenging at first, but with practice it becomes easier. Knowing how to describe the kind of beer you like is also quite useful; it is an invaluable tool when exploring a new beer menu and asking wait staff for suggestions. This tasting is about finding effective ways to describe a beer.

To prepare this tasting you need to cut out small pieces of paper, each with either the number one or the number two written on them, and put them all in a hat or bowl. You also need a sheet of paper and pen for each participant. With this tasting, two beers are served at once. The beers, like the pieces of paper, are labelled as beer number one and two. Each participant draws a number. Everyone then samples both beers, taking notes only on the aromas and flavours of the beer that corresponds with the number they drew. Once the notes are complete, sheets are exchanged and participants try to guess which of the two beers is being described on the sheet. As a ground rule, it's best to avoid the mention of colour in this tasting, as it can provide a clear indicator and spoil all the fun!

This game can be relatively easy or quite difficult, depending on how similar the two beers are. It also gets easier with every round, as players find strategic ways to describe their beers. It might be a good idea to start with easy sets and then work towards more difficult ones. I've included a few suggested pairs to get things started:

EASY

1. Irish Red Ale   2. Porter

1. Saison   2. Cream Ale

1. Belgian Pale Ale   2. American Amber Ale

1. Tripel   2. Barley Wine

CHALLENGING

1. Munich Helles   2. California Common

1. German Wheat Beer   2. Belgian Wheat Beer

1. Pilsner   2. Pale Ale

1. Bock   2. Scotch Ale

Beer Ranking Game Beer has a number of measurable attributes: Its colour can be measured by SRM (standard reference method) values and its carbonation in volumes of CO_2. Bitterness in beer is measured in IBUs (international bitterness units) and alcohol is generally measured by ABV (alcohol by volume). Beer also has a range of attributes that are not as easily quantifiable, like its level of complexity, intensity and balance.

This game is about comparing the intensity of various beer qualities. It requires no preparation. It is best done as a group or in teams because it stimulates interesting debates, but it can certainly also be enjoyed as a game of solitaire. The rules are simple: sample a range of beers and put them in order. It's particularly interesting to use the same group of beers and reorder them three or four times according to different criteria, causing people to look at the same beers under different lights.

Here are a few ranking ideas:

◆ least carbonated to most carbonated (this one should always be done first, because carbonation will dissipate with time)

◆ palest to darkest in colour

◆ driest to sweetest

◆ lighted to boldest in flavour (or least complex to most complex)

◆ least bitter to most bitter

◆ lightest to boldest in alcohol

◆ least fruity to fruitiest

◆ most typical to most unusual

"Can You Identify Your Favourite?" Tasting Despite the sea of beers that are available on the market today, a lot of people have a go-to brand. Sometimes their choice is based on flavour and sometimes it's image-based. Often, it's a combination of both. In this blind tasting, participants are challenged to see if they can pick out their favourite beer from among a large group of beers. Each guest brings their favourite beer to contribute it to the tasting.

This tasting requires a little more planning because it is conducted blind, meaning that participants should not know which beer is which. In order to avoid confusion during the tasting, it's best to mark the cups for each beer with a separate number or colour. For this tasting, it's also a good idea to use opaque cups like coffee cups or mugs to prevent easy identification based on colour. During the tasting, you will need a designated pourer in a separate room. You should also instruct each guest to bring the beers in an opaque container. Knowing which other beers are in the mix takes away from the intrigue!

A variation on this tasting is to pick up five to seven beers that are very similar in style and flavour, number the cups, provide a list and challenge guests to taste everything and guess which beer is which.

Vertical Tasting The idea of a vertical tasting comes from the wine world. It involves tasting different vintages of the same beer. Although the tasting itself is easy to organize, it does require planning over an extended period of time. A number of breweries release beers that are appropriate for cellaring (see page 11). Some of these beers are produced year-round but most of them are released as a seasonal treat once a year. In order to assemble a vertical tasting, these beers need to be collected over a period of at least two years and cellared properly. Having collected three or more bottles of the same beer at yearly intervals, it is interesting to compare them, sampling them side by side to see how the flavours in that beer have evolved over time.

It's always a good idea to research the beers in question, as some breweries like to vary the recipes of their seasonal releases, and this information is pertinent to the tasting. For those who regularly keep a cellar, it's also helpful to take written notes on how the flavours in this specific beer has evolved, trying to pinpoint the ideal (or preferred) age at which to consume it.

Horizontal Tasting Horizontal beer tastings are also inspired by the wine world. For this tasting, a series of beers from different breweries that are brewed in the same style are tasted side by side for comparison. This is a great way to identify the nuances within a certain beer style. It is surprising how these beers can be so similar and yet completely different at the same time.

This beer tasting is best conducted blind, as many people might unwittingly gravitate towards specific beers based on where or by whom they were produced. Although it's tempting to simply focus on which is the favourite beer, there are many judging parameters that can be used for horizontal tastings. Suggested parameters can be found on the facing page.

Home-vs.-Away Tasting Because beer ingredients are portable, terroir no longer dictates where individual styles of beer are brewed. A Belgian-style pale ale can be brewed in Belgium, the U.S. or Canada, or even Japan. As long as the necessary ingredients are sourced and used, the Belgian-style pale ale brewed in Japan might taste just as authentic as its Belgian counterpart. Having said this, a lot of brewers who make beer on a small scale know their customers and some choose to tweak their beer recipes, moving away from tradition to brew a beer that is better suited to local palates, preferences and foods. This tasting explores the nuances between locally brewed beers and the beers that inspired them.

This is another blind tasting, with someone pouring into numbered glasses in a separate room. Beers are brought out in pairs with one being a locally brewed example and the other being a beer of the same style brewed in its country of origin. Guests can then taste the two beers side by side and make observations. Here are some questions to assist in guiding the discussion:

? How are these two beers similar.

? How are they different.

? Does one taste fresher than the other.

? Which beer do you like most and why.

? Which one do you think is the local example.

A reveal can either be done after each pair of beers has been discussed or at the very end of the tasting. The interesting thing about doing separate reveals each time is that participants will dive into the next pairing with a notion of how local beers are different from imports and look for patterns. Doing a reveal at the end leaves people guessing, which is equally interesting. When going this route, especially when tackling three or four pairs of beers, it's best to have paper handy so that participants can keep track of their guesses.

The Belgian-style pale ale brewed in Japan might taste just as authentic as its Belgian counterpart.

Great Brewing Traditions Triangular Tasting There are four beer cultures that have shaped our current beer landscape and the majority of beers on the market today are inspired by one of these traditions. The idea behind this tasting is to zero in on the defining characteristics of each brewing culture.

The four cultures in question are the German tradition, the British tradition, the Belgian tradition and the American craft beer tradition. While there is a wide range of beer styles being brewed in these countries, the history, geography and culture of these areas have shaped their brewing traditions and influenced the conventional beer styles from that area. Keep in mind that these are generalizations, and there are many styles that fall outside these parameters. Here is a chart that will help point you in the right direction and spark discussion:

	INTENSITY	BITTERNESS	SWEETNESS	FRUIT NOTES	FLAVOURS TO LOOK OUT FOR
GERMAN	Understated	In balance	Understated	Rare	Bread crust/toast Fresh cereal grain notes Earthy notes
BRITISH	Understated	In balance	In balance	Common	Caramel notes Pear/apple/currant notes Herbal notes
BELGIAN	Bold	Understated	Present	Common	Dried and fresh fruit notes Pepper/spicy notes Funky/unusual notes
AMERICAN	Bold	Bold	In balance	Common	Citrus notes Pine/resinous notes Funky/unusual notes

One of the easiest ways to identify similarities and differences between beers is by comparing them to one another. In this case, because we are trying to zero in on general traits, as opposed to specific notes, the best thing to do is compare three samples. This type of tasting is known as a triangle taste test. Each flight consists of two beers from the same brewing tradition, and one from a different brewing tradition. The idea is to taste all three beers, see if you can identify similarities and differences, and zero in on which one of the three beers is from the different brewing tradition.

This beer tasting can be done with knowledge of which beer is which, in which case, you can ask the following questions:

? How are the two beers from the same tradition similar.

? How is the third beer different.

? Which of the three beers do you like most, and why.

? Which traits are you drawn to in that beer.

? Are those traits particular to the tradition that inspired this beer.

Alternatively, it can be conducted as a blind tasting, and with each flight the questions could be:

? How are these three beers similar.

? How are they different.

? Does one of the three stand out, or seem different.

? What sets this beer apart.

With a blind tasting, it's always good to continue the discussion after the reveal. Here are some suggested flights to get you started:

EASY

1. Saison (Belgian)	2. Tripel (Belgian)	3. IPA (American)
1. Pilsner (German)	2. Märzen (German)	3. Wheat Beer (Belgian)
1. Golden Ale (American)	2. Golden Lager (American)	3. Pale Ale (British)
1. Barley wine (British)	2. Pale Ale (British)	3. Dunkel (German)

CHALLENGING

1. Stout (British)	2. Porter (British)	3. Schwarzbier (German)
1. Bock (German)	2. Dunkel (German)	3. Scotch Ale (British)
1. IPA (American)	2. Imperial Stout (American)	3. Tripel (Belgian)
1. Dubbel (Belgian)	2. Saison (Belgian)	3. Traditional Bock (German)

WHY BOTHER PAIRING BEER WITH FOOD?

In North America, there are many who still view the idea of bringing beer to the table as being new and unusual. Although there are beer enthusiasts, brewers and restaurants that have been championing beer and food pairing for years, it has remained a niche interest. This is quite unfortunate, because pairing beer with food can easily yield delicious results. For those who enjoy food and find delight in discovering new flavours, including beer among potential accompaniments for meals adds a whole new dimension to the dining experience.

The concept of pairing beer with food is far from revolutionary. There are parts of the world where beer has been consumed at the table for hundreds of years. In countries that lie in the northern European grain belt, like Belgium and England, beer has historically been more accessible than wine and, as a result, is more commonly found at the table. As a consequence, and because brewers have quite a bit of flexibility in how they design their beers, a number of traditional beer styles from these areas are well suited to pair with local foods there (see sidebar on page 123).

If you want to venture away from traditional pairings, there are countless tasty beer and food combinations to discover and explore. There really is a beer for every food and a food for every beer. Beer can add depth to a five-course meal, enhance the delicate notes in a crisp salad, highlight subtle flavours in a range of cheeses, complement the complex notes in chocolate or simply counterbalance a salty snack. Beer is just as at home at the pub as it is in a restaurant; it's simply a matter of finding the right one for the occasion.

So why is it that pairing beer with food appears to be a new trend in North America? In large part, it is because, in the years after Prohibition, North America saw a consolidation of its breweries, followed by a dramatic reduction in the number of beers on the market. For a period of twenty to thirty years, depending on the area, the vast majority of beers available were golden in colour, in the 4–5% ABV range and highly carbonated. While these beers pair well with certain foods, they don't provide a palette of flavours to work with. Consider how popular it would be to pair wine with food if the only wines available were red, full-bodied and jammy, with an ABV around 13–15%. Finding the right beer to pair with any given food requires a selection of beers from which to choose.

Thankfully, with an increase in imports and the emergence of the craft beer movement in the latter half of the twentieth century, there is now a wide spectrum of beer flavours. In fact, the beer world provides a greater breadth of flavours than there is in the wine world. Beer can have an alcohol content that ranges from under 2% ABV up into the sphere of fortified wines and even higher. It can include sweet, bitter, sour, salty and umami flavours in any combination. It is made from four basic ingredients, each of which contributes its own aromas and flavours. Furthermore, within each of these four components, there is a lot of room for variation and nuance, not to mention the possibility of incorporating additional ingredients.

While finding a spectacular pairing might require some trial and error, finding a good one is relatively easy. This is because the basic flavours in beer are relatable and direct parallels can be made between these flavours and some of the flavours found in food. The malt used to brew beer, for example, is cooked to varying degrees. A beer made from lightly kilned malts will have fresh-bread or grain flavours that will tie in nicely with a baguette sandwich. A beer made with roasted malts, meanwhile, will have dark chocolate or coffee notes; most people intuitively know which foods will work well with those flavours.

A word of caution: many who are familiar with wine pairing might instinctively default to pairing traditional foods with beers that are brewed in their region of origin. Although this can work in the case of long-established beer styles that are still brewed in their original loca-

There is now a wide spectrum of beer flavours— providing a greater breadth of flavour than wine.

tion, it is important to note that, because beer ingredients are portable, the style in which a beer was brewed is more relevant than where it was brewed. For example, a Belgian-style tripel brewed in Japan will likely provide a better pairing for a Belgian eel dish than a common lager that was brewed in Belgium.

The best departure point when choosing a beer to pair with food is its flavour profile or style description. It is, of course, always best to have the opportunity to taste the beer and become familiar with its nuances before settling on the foods to pair it with. When faced with choosing from among a row of sealed bottles at the store, however, those who are familiar with styles can make reasonable assumptions about which beer will be the best fit based on the listed style as well as the alcohol content or other information that might be present on the label.

Classic Beer and Food Pairings from the Grain Belt

Country	Eat	Drink
England	Oysters	Stout
	Ploughman's lunch	Pale ale
	Steak-and-kidney pie	Porter
Germany	Weisswurst sausage	Bavarian wheat beer
	Roasted duck	Oktoberfest lager
	Mettwurst sausage	Kölsch
Belgium	Escavèche marinated fish	Tripel
	Fresh brown shrimp	Flanders red-brown
	Pottekeis open cheese sandwich	Gueuze

With a little practice, pairing beer with food quickly becomes instinctive. Taking a moment to consider what you're eating before choosing a beer will enhance the enjoyment of both the food and the beer. The character of beer can meld seamlessly with the flavours in food, heighten the perception of individual tones or bring out nuances that weren't apparent before; at times, the combination of beer and food can even result in a completely new and unexpected note. Sometimes, the flavours don't meld at all, but instead dance back and forth in a succession of fleeting notes. In any case, it's usually an enjoyable experience.

HOW TO PAIR BEER WITH FOOD Pairing beer with food is delightful. This section outlines some basic rules and guidelines that will provide a good departure point for beginners as well as some insight for those who have identified or stumbled upon favourite beer-and-food combinations and are curious to know why they work.

Pairing beer with food is an art that is full of nuances. Those who are familiar with wine pairing will know that so-called pairing rules can sometimes be misleading. Sweeping statements like "Pair chicken only with beverage X" are limiting and close the door to a number of pairing opportunities, not to mention the fact that this type of rule doesn't take preparation into account. A steamed chicken breast, for example, won't call for the same type of beverage as General Tso's chicken, jerk chicken or Southern fried chicken. It is always best to pay attention on the dish at hand instead of indiscriminately following a set of broad rules.

When pairing beer with food, it's a good idea to focus first on the dominant flavour in the dish. This will sometimes be the protein, but it can also be the sauce or seasoning. From there, a lot of fine-tuning can be done to perfect the pairing. What constitutes a successful pairing depends on the individual. As a general rule, the flavours of both the food and the beer should still be apparent and preferably highlighted. From there, personal preference will dictate which individual flavours should be accented. For example, someone who enjoys bitterness will

not want the hoppy finish of a beer to be lost in the pairing, whereas someone who isn't keen on bitterness might gravitate towards a pairing that subdues that aspect of the beer, and brings out its other qualities.

Flavour interactions can be quite complex. Sometimes a sweet note in beer will coax out a sweet note in the food and sometimes it will obliterate it. In the same way, a bitter note in beer might provide a lovely contrast to a sweeter dish or it might stick out and become distracting. In both cases, the result depends on the intensity of that one note within the beer or food's overall character as well as the other notes or elements that are present in both items. With practice, it becomes easier to predict these various subtle interactions. Beer pairing is not an exact science, but rather a gustatory adventure.

The best way to zero in on a perfect pairing is by sampling a range of combinations. Of course, understanding the basics of food pairing theory is helpful. Having said this, because beer is such a complex and multilayered beverage, there are many beer and food combinations that are fantastic despite the fact that they do not conform to pairing recommendations at all. It's therefore always a good idea to experiment and play, opening the palate to the possibility of unexpectedly delightful flavour interactions.

BEER AND FOOD PAIRING GUIDELINES

Intensity When pairing food with a beverage of any sort, it is important to consider intensity. The intensity of the beer should be in line with the intensity of the dish at hand. This is essentially common sense. If a green salad is paired with a high-alcohol Russian imperial stout that has bold coffee and dried-fruit notes, it will be difficult to taste the salad. On the opposite side of the spectrum, if a rich beef and vegetable stew is paired with a lite lager, it might as well have been paired with water because the delicate character of the beer will be completely eclipsed by the food.

Being mindful of intensity is a key in any pairing and this is the one guideline in this section that might best be considered as a rule. It is important not to lose sight of it while exploring the various flavour interactions outlined below. Of course, rules can be broken. Having said this, breaking this particular one rarely yields positive results.

Most people have a firm grasp on how intense various food items are. Here are four elements that affect the intensity of beer.

Alcohol Content It is pretty safe to assume that a beer that is very high in alcohol will have a more intense flavour profile than one that is lower in alcohol. In a pinch, consulting the alcohol content stated on the bottle can suffice. There are, however, other nuances that affect the overall intensity of a beer.

Body A beer with a fuller body will seem more intense than a light-bodied one. While body and alcohol content often go hand in hand, there are some exceptions. Within the spectrum of high-alcohol beers, for example, a 9% ABV Belgian tripel will generally have a lighter body than a barley wine of the same strength.

Flavour Some beer flavours—bitterness for example—are perceived as being more intense than others. When these flavours are prominent in a beer, the beer itself will often seem more intense. A classic example of this are stouts, which are often thought of as heavy despite the fact that their alcohol content and body are in the average range. This may be due in part to their dark, opaque colour, but it is also because they have bold, roasted aromas and flavours of bitter coffee.

Complexity A complex layering of flavours can overwhelm the senses and increase the perceived intensity of a beer. It is often suggested, as a helpful hint for those familiar with wine pairings, to choose an ale when a dish calls for red wine and a lager where a white wine might be used. This broad statement relates, in part, to complexity. An ale will generally be more complex than a lager of equal strength and therefore better suited to pair with fuller-flavoured or more complex foods.

Flavour Interactions Each beer has its own specific and often intricate assemblage of flavours. When aligned with the dominant note and underlying components in the dish, these flavours provide the building blocks for each individual pairing. This section includes some of the more easily identifiable components that might be present in a dish's flavour profile, outlining how each of these components should be addressed when choosing a complementary beer.

The Basics The first step when zeroing in on a pairing is finding a beer with notes that resonate with those in the dish at hand. Assuming the intensity lines up, identifying one or two resonant elements generally result in a good pairing.

Sweetness If the dominant note in the dish is sweet, the beer should be as sweet as, if not sweeter than, the dish, otherwise the sweetness in the food can eliminate the perception of sweetness in the beer, overemphasizing its bitter finish. Sweetness in beer will, in turn, tone down the perception of sweetness in the dish, allowing other nuances to shine through.

Saltiness If the dominant note in the dish is salty, the beer should be lower in alcohol with a soft sweetness and a moderate or high level of bitterness. Salt lessens the perception of bitterness and emphasizes the sweeter notes in the beer. The sweetness in the beer, meanwhile, will tone down the salt in the overall profile of the dish. A lower alcohol content makes it more comfortable to wash away residual salt with large mouthfuls of beer, and prevents the development of sharp alcohol notes that salt can bring out in high-alcohol beer. *Note:* Salt also tones down the perception of acidity in a sour beer.

Sourness If the dominant note in the dish is sour, the beer should have a soft sweetness or noticeable fruity notes. Acidity in food will emphasize the sweeter tones and enliven fruit notes in beer. If the sweetness in the beer is bold, however, it can throw the balance of the dish by overshadowing any underlying sweetness, leaving only a sour note. *Note*: A beer with a slight acidity will also provide a lovely complement to sour food.

Spiciness If the dominant note in the dish is a spicy heat, the beer should have a noticeable bitterness. Bitterness causes salivation, which will help temporarily relieve the accumulative sensation of heat that spicy food produces in the mouth.

Bitterness Should a bold bitterness be present in the dish, the accompanying beer should have a low bitterness. Bitterness in food compounds the bitter finish of a beer and, combined, they can reach distracting levels. *Note*: A beer with a slight acidity will also be a lovely complement to bitter food.

Umami Umami is an elusive and intricate taste. Should a bold umami taste be present in the dish, the accompanying beer should have umami notes as well. Research has found that combining different types of umami heightens the overall perception of it. *Note*: A beer with a slight acidity will also heighten the perception of umami in food.

Aromatic Flavour Elements If specific aromatic flavour elements are present in the dish, look for beers with parallel or complementary notes. There are many aromas and flavours that can be present both in beer and in food. Some examples are bread, toast, honey, caramel, toffee, coffee or chocolate, as well as a wide range of fruit, spice and herbal notes. Finding parallel flavours in beer and food can result in a lovely pairing. Bringing together complementary flavours—for example pairing a beer with a dominant coffee-like note with a dessert item—can also yield delightful results.

Fine-Tuning Beer is a multifaceted beverage. Beyond making sure that intensity and character are in harmony with the dish, consider the secondary flavour elements in beer in order to fine-tune the match by providing balance or contrast. Here is a list of beer traits that can add dimension to a range of pairings.

Taste

Bitterness Bitterness in beer can be used to balance sweet notes in food. It also does a great job of breaking through foods that have a rich, creamy texture.

Sweetness Sweetness in beer can be used to tone down the perception of salty notes in food. It can also be used to counterbalance and attenuate the sensation of heat in spicy food.

Acidity The acidity in sour beers can provide a sharp contrast to highlight the unctuousness of umami-rich foods. Like bitterness, acidity can also be used to cut through foods with a rich, creamy texture.

Mouthfeel

Carbonation Carbonation in beer is accompanied by a soft acidity. Highly carbonated beer is therefore a great accompaniment for rich and fatty foods, because the combination of acidity and bubbles will help break through oils and cleanse the palate between bites. Different levels and types of carbonation also affect the texture of beer. These nuances in texture can be used to complement or contrast the texture of food.

Alcohol High alcohol levels in beer can result in sharp flavours as well as a sensation of heat. Alcohol notes can be used to counterbalance and cut through foods with a rich texture. In particular, high-alcohol beers tend to fare well with dessert items, since a higher alcohol content in beer is often accompanied by a certain degree of sweetness.

Dryness Some beers have a dry mouthfeel that can be a result of either hard water or tannins. This dry texture provides a pleasant contrast to oily foods.

Temperature The ideal serving temperature varies with each beer (see page 15). It can be interesting to take these different temperatures into account when fine-tuning pairings.

Potential Pitfalls While pairing beer with food rarely results in a blatant clash of flavours, there are two elements in beer that have a potential for causing dissonance within the pairing.

Hops Hops can react with a variety of fish and shellfish, resulting in an unpleasant metallic note. It is therefore best to be cautious when pairing hoppy beers with seafood.

Alcohol Alcohol can compound the sensation of heat. It is therefore not advisable to pair high-alcohol beers with spicy food.

Mirella's Rule of Thumb

In experimenting with beer and food pairing, I've developed a general rule that I feel can provide a useful departure point when picking a beer to pair with any given dish: line up the depth of colour of the beer with the colour of the main ingredient in the dish. In other words, use a golden beer with chicken or white fish dishes; an amber beer with turkey, pork and root vegetables; a brown beer for beans or steak; and black beer for chocolate cake. This approach seems to work most of the time. Of course, it is simply one aspect of the pairing, because within each of these colour families exists a wide spectrum of beers that vary in intensity and flavour.

THE NOTION OF PAIRING BEER with food is even more delightful when it is explored in good company. Because the concept of bringing beer to the table is still new to many people, it is a great way to spice up a dinner or informal gathering. Whether the pairings are perfect or not, they are likely to spark stimulating and lively conversation.

ENTERTAINING WITH BEER

HOSTING A BEER DINNER

When making beer the star at a dinner party, there are limitless pairing possibilities. For a first foray into beer dining, focus on a series of familiar or favourite dishes so that more time and attention can be spent on selecting the accompanying beers for each course.

Try to aim for three to five courses in order to avoid overwhelming the palate with too many flavour combinations. As with beer tastings, it's also a good idea to monitor total alcohol intake. Generally serving four- to five-ounce (120–150 mL) pours of each beer works well, depending on the alcohol content of the beers and the total number of beers served. It is also best to start with lighter-flavoured beers and work towards more intense flavours. This should occur naturally, since appetizers tend to be lighter than dessert and the intensity of the beers used should line up with the intensity of each dish. For additional serving tips, see page 15.

From there, many different themes can be explored in the context of a beer dinner. It's possible to start with the beers, choosing a few favourite brews and building a menu around them. It can be interesting to focus on the beers of one specific brewery, pairing a course with each of their different brands. Beer dinners can also explore a series of traditional pairings from classic beer-producing regions like Belgium or Germany. In areas where there is a thriving craft beer scene, it is fun to create a menu that pairs local seasonal beers with foods that are also in season. The possibilities are endless.

BEEROLOGY BEER AND CHEESE Planning a beer and cheese tasting party is less involved than a beer dinner and provides an entertaining twist on the classic wine and cheese reception. Beer is a fantastic companion for cheese. Its lower alcohol content and carbonation are a great foil for salt and oils, both of which are often present in cheese. In addition to this, a number of the flavours that are common in cheese will mirror those in beer, resulting in seamless pairings.

There are many ways to plan a beer and cheese party. The pairings can be pre-arranged using beer and food pairing theory. In this scenario guests all sit together with a cheese plate and corresponding series of beers. Each pairing is enjoyed in sequence and discussed. It's also entertaining to simply assemble a cheese board and offer a selection of beers, inviting guests to choose a beer and enjoy it with a range of different cheeses. Beer and cheese go so well together that mixing and matching often yields a surprising array of successful pairing, each of which reveals a different series of flavour interactions.

The flavours present in cheese are quite varied, so the beers should be as well. What follows is a suggested selection of seven beer styles that, when assembled, should provide enough flavour variation to pair with a broad range of cheeses. Accompanying cheese varieties are also proposed. These suggestions are meant as a departure point to spark dialogue, keeping in mind that within each of the listed beer and cheese categories there is a large potential for variation in character, texture and flavour.

Beer and cheese

- ◆ **Golden ale:** for fresh cheeses and mildly flavoured hard cheeses.
- ◆ **Wheat beer:** for mild bloomy-rind cheeses and mild goat's-milk cheese.
- ◆ **Amber or dark ale:** for cheeses with nutty flavours and mild sheep's-milk cheese.
- ◆ **Farmhouse ale:** for soft washed-rind cheese and bolder bloomy-rind cheeses.
- ◆ **Porter or stout:** for cheeses with sweet caramel tones and dry, salty cheeses.
- ◆ **Pale ale:** for medium-aged cheeses and firm washed-rind cheeses.
- ◆ **Strong ale:** for sharp-flavoured aged hard cheeses and blue cheeses.

BEEROLOGY BEER AND CHOCOLATE TASTING PARTY

While the pairings for a beer and chocolate tasting party can certainly be planned, a less formal format lends itself particularly well to this decadent combination. It can be as effortless as splitting a beer with friends and diving into a box of chocolates together to find the best possible pairing.

Pairing beer with chocolate may seem outlandish but it can yield delicious results. As with cheese, the carbonation in beer will help cleanse the rich coating that each piece of chocolate leaves behind, helping to refresh the palate between every bite. It also provides a delightful textural contrast to the chocolate itself. Flavour-wise, a parallel can be drawn between the characters of beer and chocolate as they both strike a balance between sweet and bitter notes. Many styles of beer can be successfully paired with chocolate, but there are certain characteristics and styles that are particularly well suited for a beer and chocolate tasting party. Here are some suggestions to assist in launching a beer and chocolate pairing exploration.

Dark Beers Dark beers are brewed with roasted grains that impart dark chocolate and coffee notes. The roasted flavours in these beers mirror cocoa notes in milk chocolate, but are bitter enough to cut through its richer tones.

American Pale Ales The bitterness in American pale ales can provide a lovely contrast to the rich notes in milk chocolate. The hop character in these beers can also contribute bold fruit flavours that will be intensified through the pairing.

High-Alcohol Beers High-alcohol beers have a complex flavour profile, fuller body and warming quality. These qualities make them a particularly delightful pairing for dark chocolate, providing a lovely textural contrast and nuanced interplay of flavours.

Fruit Beers Beers with bold fruit flavours pair well with a range of chocolates, mimicking, complementing or paralleling the flavours of fruit fillings, depending on the piece of chocolate at hand.

Amber Beers These often have notes of caramel, toffee or nuts that parallel the delicate flavours in white chocolate. Sweeter pieces of white chocolate fare well with lower-alcohol styles while richer ones pair well with higher alcohol, amber-coloured beers.

Beer and chocolate

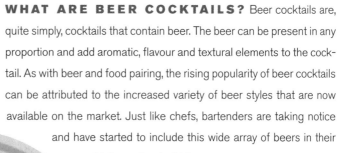

WHAT ARE BEER COCKTAILS? Beer cocktails are, quite simply, cocktails that contain beer. The beer can be present in any proportion and add aromatic, flavour and textural elements to the cocktail. As with beer and food pairing, the rising popularity of beer cocktails can be attributed to the increased variety of beer styles that are now available on the market. Just like chefs, bartenders are taking notice and have started to include this wide array of beers in their cocktail creation tool kit.

Some classic examples of mixed drinks containing beer are the shandy and Radler that usually bring together beer and citrus-flavoured soda or lemonade; the snakebite, which is beer and cider; and the black velvet, which blends stout with champagne. Many have also sampled beer mixes, like a half and half, or enjoyed a beer into which a shot of spirit was dropped—this melding technique is known as a depth charge.

The current wave of beer cocktails is a little more involved than the mixed drinks listed above. Like traditional cocktails, these beer cocktails combine spirits, mixers and other flavouring ingredients; they can be shaken, stirred or built and are generally served in smaller glasses. The addition of beer will contribute distinct aromas and flavours to the mix, as well as carbonation.

A FEW BASIC TIPS ON CREATING COCKTAILS

The whole idea behind adding beer to a cocktail is to use the character of that particular beer to contribute an added dimension. The beer should therefore be detectable in the finished cocktail, either as a distinct note or as an indefinable component of the overall flavour profile.

When creating a beer cocktail, it is therefore best to start with the flavour of the beer itself. A great first step is to simply taste the beer that will be used and try to zero in on which particular spirit or mixers might best complement it. From there, with a little trial and error, it is possible to pinpoint the correct combination and proportion of ingredients. Here are a few tips to keep in mind when designing and mixing beer cocktails.

1. Carbonation is a delightful attribute. It is best to combine the cocktail in a way that will not disrupt its natural effervescence, so pour gently and stir the beer as little as possible. Another way to help preserve carbonation is by cooling the glass and other ingredients before bringing them in contact with the beer, because contact with warmer temperatures will cause the beer to foam.

2. Keep in mind the alcohol content of the beer when determining the portions and total amount of spirits in the cocktail. It's easy to slip into thinking of beer simply as a mixer.

3. When re-creating a cocktail with a different brand of beer, it is a good idea to taste along, and be aware that small changes will likely have to be made to the recipe in order to achieve the original balance of flavours. Of course, this also applies when using a new make of spirits or mixers.

4. Be aware that cream-based liqueurs and milk or cream will often curdle when they come into contact with beer. Proceed with caution.

5. This should go without saying: beer can be stirred, but should absolutely not be shaken!

CUCUMBER PILS

This summery cocktail brings together the fresh flavours of cucumber and lime with herbal notes from both gin and pilsner. The resulting combination of flavours takes the refreshing nature of pilsner to a whole new level!

1 1/2 thick slices of cucumber
    (peeled)
1 tsp (5 mL) granulated sugar
1/2 tsp (2 mL) lime juice
    (juice of half a lime)
1/2 ounce (15 mL) gin
2 1/2 ounces (75 mL) pilsner*
cucumber wheel for garnish

Cut the cucumber slices into thin strips. Muddle the cucumber, sugar and lime juice at the bottom of an 8-ounce (240 mL) rocks glass. Add gin and stir. Half-fill the glass with ice. Gently pour in the pilsner and garnish with a cucumber wheel.

*can also be made with common lager

Cucumber Pils

WITTY SHOT

This lively little shot of beer is like a fruit salad in a glass, but with bubbles!

1/4 ounce (7 mL) peach schnapps
1/8 ounce (3 mL) melon liqueur
dash of lime
dash of Belgian wheat beer

In a shot glass, combine the schnapps, melon liqueur and a dash of lime. Top up with Belgian style wheat beer.

MOUSTACHE

This cocktail is playfully called a "moustache" because its elegant look and robust flavours are reminiscent of classic cocktails of the late nineteenth century, a time when it was fashionable for men to sport moustaches.

1/4 ounce (7 mL) Canadian whisky
1/4 ounce (7 mL) sweet red vermouth
4 1/2 ounces (135 mL) Vienna lager
orange twist for garnish

Blend the whisky and vermouth in a shaker with ice. Put a handful of ice cubes in an 8-ounce (240 mL) rocks glass (it should be one-quarter full). Pour in the whisky and vermouth. Gently add the Vienna lager and stir. Garnish with an orange twist.

RYESCAPADE

This decadent cocktail brings together two Canadian classics, ice wine and rye (Canadian whisky). These ingredients blend seamlessly with the beer, resulting in a sumptuous cocktail that reveals a new nuance of flavour with every sip.

> **sugar for the rim**
> **1/2 ounce (15 mL) Canadian whisky**
> **1 ounce (30 mL) ice wine**
> **3 1/2 ounces (100 mL) Bavarian**
> **wheat beer**
> **lemon twist for garnish**

Rim a 6-ounce (180 mL) martini glass with sugar. Shake the whisky and ice wine together and strain into the glass. Gently add the Bavarian wheat beer. Garnish with a lemon twist.

Ryescapade

FANCY GOAT

This cocktail is a playful anachronism, pulling the current trend of beer cocktails back to the days of the very first book ever published on bartending, in which a number of cocktails were listed as having "old-fashioned," "plain," "fancy" or "improved" variations.

1/2 tsp (2 mL) Cointreau
1/4 tsp (1 mL) simple syrup
2 dashes of bitters
2 ounces (60 mL) bock
lemon twist for garnish

Shake the Cointreau, simple syrup and bitters and strain into a 6-ounce (180 mL) martini glass. Gently add the bock and garnish with a lemon twist.

BB SOUR

This cocktail is inspired by sour beers. It is a deconstruction of sorts, bringing together the malty tones of English brown ale with the barrel-aged characteristics in bourbon as well as sour notes from the grapefruit and lemon.

1/2 ounce (15 mL) bourbon
1 ounce (30 mL) grapefruit juice
1/4 tsp (1 mL) simple syrup
dash of lemon
4 ounces (120 mL) English brown ale
lemon wedge for garnish

Stir the bourbon, grapefruit juice, simple syrup and lemon. Strain into an 8-ounce (240 mL) rocks glass and add two or three ice cubes. Gently add the brown ale. Throw in the lemon wedge.

Italiano

ITALIANO

Inspired by the classic Campari-based Americano cocktail, this drink turns the tables, spicing up a classic American style of beer and taking it into traditional Italian cocktail territory.

1/2 ounce (15 mL) ruby port
1 ounce (30 mL) Campari
1 ounce (30 mL) orange juice
dash of bitters
5 ounces (150 mL) American pale ale
grapefruit twist for garnish

Fill a 12-ounce (355 mL) highball glass with 1/2 cup (125 mL) crushed ice. Add the port, Campari, orange juice, bitters and beer and stir gently. Garnish with a grapefruit twist.

T.T.

The Tropical Tripel cocktail is inspired by the fruity notes in tripels. It is playfully conceived as a warm-weather vacation in a glass for those who reside in cooler climates, perhaps behind monastery walls.

   1/4 ounce (7 mL) Malibu
        coconut-flavoured rum
   1/4 tsp (1 mL) crème de banane
   1 ounce (30 mL) pineapple juice
   3 1/2 ounces (100 mL) tripel
   1/2 ounce (15 mL) spiced rum
   pineapple pieces for garnish

Shake the Malibu, crème de banane and pineapple juice, and strain them into a 6-ounce (180 mL) champagne flute. Very gently, pour in the tripel. Float the spiced rum on top and garnish.

T.T.

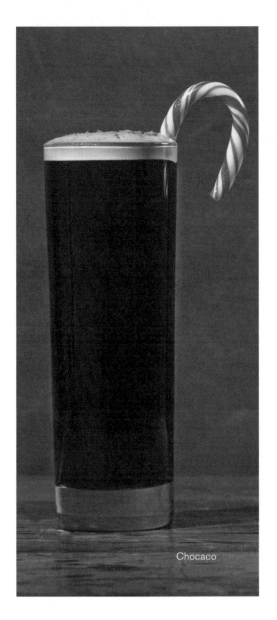

Chocaco

CHOCACO

The Chocolate Candy Cane Cocktail—Chocaco for short—celebrates candy canes, balancing their bright mint character with richer chocolate and coffee tones, resulting in a festive cocktail that will spice up any winter holiday gathering.

1 ounce (30 mL) dark rum
1/2 ounce (15 mL) dark crème de cacao
1 tsp (5 mL) white crème de menthe
splash of red food colouring* (optional)
8 1/2 ounces (250 mL) stout
candy cane and cocoa for garnish

Combine the rum, crème de cacao, crème de menthe and food colouring in a shaker half full of ice. Strain into a 12-ounce (355 mL) Collins glass. Gently add the stout and stir. Garnish with a candy cane and a sprinkle of cocoa.

Depending on the stout used, red food colouring will lend its colour to the foam.

PART FOUR

Glossary & Tools

A GLOSSARY OF TERMS

ABV: Alcohol by volume—a measure of the alcohol, or ethanol, content in an alcoholic beverage, expressed as a percentage of the total volume of the beverage.

ABW: Alcohol by weight—an expression of the ethanol content in an alcoholic beverage. Stated as a percentage of the total weight of the beverage as opposed to a percentage of the total volume.

acetaldehyde: A compound that can be found in beer. It is usually described as having a green apple or cider-like character. Produced in the early stages of fermentation, acetaldehyde can some-times be detected at very low levels in finished beers, most commonly in golden lagers. When the acetaldehyde note in a beer is strong, it is considered to be a brewing fault.

Acetobacter: A bacteria that converts alcohol into acetic acid. Among other things, it is the bacteria responsible for turning wine or beer into vinegar.

adjunct: Anything (besides malted grain) that is added to beer as a fermentable ingredient for the yeast to convert into alcohol. Examples include corn, rice and sugar.

alpha acid: Resinous hop compounds that, once they are boiled and dissolved, will contribute bitterness to beer.

Altbier: A style of beer associated with Düsseldorf and northern Germany. When lager yeast became popular in Germany, most breweries switched their production, leaving ale recipes behind. Altbier is one of the few ale styles that persisted. The term *alt* means "old" and refers to the fact that these beers are brewed the old way. A classic example of this style would be Uerige Alt.

attenuation: Refers to the percentage of sugars in a beer have that been consumed by the yeast. A well-attenuated or highly attenuated beer is dry.

autolysis: The self-digestion of yeast when it is unhealthy. Most commonly encountered in aged bottle-conditioned beers, autolysis contributes a character that is often described as meaty or soy-like.

Belgian lace: See lacing.

bière de mars: A historical style. In Belgium, bière de Mars was a very low-alcohol lambic beer released in the spring, *mars* meaning "March." In France, however, bière de mars is a bold version of bière de garde (see page 90). Contemporary North American examples are usually brewed in the French style.

body: Refers to the perceived weight, or thickness of beer in the mouth; it can range from light and watery to thick and chewy.

bottle-conditioned: Describes a beer that has

undergone a secondary fermentation in the bottle. Most common in Belgian-style ales and home-brewed beers. Yeast and sometimes sugar or sweet wort are added at the time of bottling. The yeast eventually settles to the bottom of the bottle. It can either be mixed back into the beer by swirling or left behind with a careful pour, depending on personal preference.

bottom-fermented beer: Lager.

Brett: Abbreviation of *Brettanomyces*, which is a type of yeast (see pages 103–4).

butterscotch: See **diacetyl.**

CAMRA: The Campaign for Real Ale, a grassroots organization founded in the U.K. in 1971 to help preserve the tradition of serving cask-conditioned ale.

cask: A keg-like container from which cask-conditioned ale is served.

cask-conditioned ale: Beer served in the traditional British way. The beer is conditioned in the vessel from which it is served, meaning that the beer finishes fermenting in the cask (see above) and is naturally carbonated. This beer is neither filtered nor pasteurized and has a very short shelf life once the cask is tapped. Cask-conditioned ale is easily recognizable at the pub because it is served using a hand pump.

chill haze: Refers to cloudiness that manifests itself in a beer at lower temperatures but then clears as the beer warms. This is usually caused by suspended protein particles in the beer. It is a superficial concern and does not generally affect the aroma and flavour of the beer.

conditioning: The later stages of fermentation. Once the yeast has consumed most of the sugars, it continues to work, breaking down undesirable aromatic and flavour compounds and then settling out of the beer.

coolship: A large, shallow open-top vessel used in the early days of brewing to cool wort between the boil and the fermentation. Most modern breweries use faster, more sanitary refrigerated cooling methods, because as wort sits in the coolship, it is vulnerable to wild yeast and bacterial contamination. This type of vessel is still used occasionally, most notably to inoculate wort for spontaneously fermented beers.

coopering: Making or repairing wooden barrels.

copper: British term for a brewing kettle.

craft brewery: A term that encompasses brewpubs, nanobreweries and microbreweries as well as breweries that are larger in size but still brew a range of different styles using traditional ingredients. There is no legal definition for the term, although the American Brewers Association has crafted a standard one.

decoction: A mashing technique that was developed in Eastern Europe because locally available ingredients yielded poor enzymatic activity. Decoction involves drawing off a part of the wort and boiling it. Some brewers will still use this technique to add dimension to lagers.

diacetyl: A compound in beer that is often described as having butterscotch or a buttered popcorn character. Diacetyl is a natural by-product of fermentation, and ale yeasts in particular can leave some behind in the final beer. When present at low levels, diacetyl can add a lovely complexity to beer but at higher levels it is considered to be a brewing fault. It is important to note that some bacteria will also produce diacetyl; it can be a symptom of dirty draught lines.

DMS: Dimethyl sulphide is a compound in beer that is derived from the malt and is commonly described as having a canned-corn character. It can be detected at low levels in some common lagers and ales. Should it be present in high concentrations in these styles or noticeable in other beers, it is considered to be a brewing fault.

Dortmunder: A golden-coloured lager style associated with the German city of Dortmund. A classic example of this style would be DAB.

double: See **imperial.**

dry-hopped: A beer to which hops were added after the boil (either in a hop back, in the fermenter or in the cask) in order to impart additional fresh hop flavours and aromas.

esters: Compounds produced by the yeast that contribute a range of fruity notes to beer. Most commonly found in ales, these compounds usually contribute a lovely complexity to these beers. When out of place, however, esters can be considered a brewing fault.

faro: Traditionally a sweetened (and sometimes spiced) light-alcohol lambic or blend of lambic and another beer. Nowadays faro is usually a sweet-ened blend of lambic beers in the 4–5% ABV range.

fining: The addition of a collagen-based clarifying agent to beer. Most commonly used in cask-conditioned beer (see page 151). Most fining agents are not suitable for a vegetarian diet.

first runnings: See **parti-gyle brewing.**

Flanders brown ale: A brown ale from Belgium found in the BJCP style guidelines, known in Belgium as Flanders old brown ales. There is some confusion between this style and the Flanders red-brown ale (categorized as a Flanders red by the BJCP) because the Flanders red-brown ale (see page 81) is often brown in colour and some Belgian examples are labelled as *oud bruin*, meaning "old brown." This style is not oak-aged and presents richer dried-fruit notes as well as molasses, coffee or chocolate notes. A classic example of this style would be Liefmans Goudenband.

flavour: An overall impression that combines aroma, taste and texture.

flight of beer: A group of beers that are tasted together.

flocculation: When yeast clumps together and falls to the bottom of the tank at the end of fermentation. Ale yeasts can also flocculate and float up to the top of the beer.

FOB: An acronym for foam on beer, FOB refers to the action of stimulating foam production in finished beer. This is done in the brewery at the time of packaging, to push oxygen out of each bottle before it is sealed. The term also refers to a piece of equipment that is used in bars to stop the flow of beer to the tap when a keg is empty.

Foeder: A large oak vessel used for conditioning and aging. It can hold thousands of gallons of beer.

Gose: A German style of ale most commonly associated with the city of Leipzig. Gose is a wheat beer brewed with coriander and salt.

Grätzer: See **grodziskie.**

grodziskie: A Polish beer style, known as Grätzer in Germany. Grodziskie is an ale made from smoked wheat malt.

gushing: Production of foam in a dramatic and uncontrollable fashion by a beer.

hop back: A piece of brewing equipment filled with hop flowers, through which the wort passes on its way out of the kettle.

IBU: International bitterness unit, a measurement of bitterness in beer.

imperial: An adjective that some brewers use to denote any beer that is stronger in alcohol than is usual for its style. This use of the word is derived from the name of the Russian imperial stout style. Other brewers prefer to use the term *double* instead.

Kellerbier: A German beer style that is served unfiltered. Traditional examples are low in carbonation as they are served directly from the vessel in which they were conditioned. This style is also sometimes referred to as Zwickelbier.

lacing: Lace-like patterns that are created by residual foam on the inside walls of a glass as a beer is consumed.

Lactobacillus: A family of bacteria that convert sugar into lactic acid.

liquor: The term brewers use to designate brewing water, in order to distinguish it from water used for other purposes, such as cleaning.

mead: An alcoholic beverage made from honey. Mead is not beer!

microbrewery: A smaller craft brewery.

nanobrewery: A term coined to describe licensed breweries that are tiny in size, only producing enough beer to regularly occupy a few taps.

nitrogen: A gas sometimes used in conjunction with carbon dioxide to carbonate beer as well as to push it through beer lines.

noble hops: A classification used for aromatic Continental European hop varieties. It conventionally refers to Hallertauer Mittelfrüh, Spalt and Tettnang hops from Germany, as well as Czech Saaz.

nucleation sites: In the context of beer glassware, tiny imperfections on the inside walls of the glass (usually scratches, etching or dirt particles) whose rough surfaces encourage carbonation to break out of solution, causing tiny bubbles to emerge and sometimes escape in a narrow stream.

old ale: A British style listed in both the BJCP and Brewers Association style guidelines. These ales are considered to be similar in style to barley wines but generally present less hop bitterness. The character of these beers is defined by prolonged aging, which can also result in sour or musty notes.

oxidation: Unpleasant aromas and flavours that develop as a beer ages. Oxidization is aggravated if the beer is in contact with oxygen and will be precipitated if the beer is stored at warmer temperatures. Oxidized flavours in beer can range from wet cardboard, to rotten fruit, to sherry-like.

parti-gyle brewing: A brewing technique that involves making two beers from the same mash. A first, more concentrated portion of wort is extracted (first runnings) and brewed into a strong beer. The grains are then re-steeped, resulting in a second portion of wort (second runnings)—which is more diluted due to a combination of sparging (see page 8) and a lower sugar content remaining in the grains. This second wort is then drawn off and brewed into a beer that is similar in character but weaker.

pasteurization: Exposure to intense heat for a short period in order to kill any potential harmful microorganisms and extend the beer's shelf life.

Pediococcus: A bacteria in the *Lactobacillus* family.

phenols: Compounds that contribute a range of notes to beer, most commonly clove, pepper, plastic and smoke. These notes will add a pleasant complexity to beer when present at low levels.

When out of place, they are considered to be a brewing fault.

real ale: A term popularized by CAMRA (see page 151) to designate cask-conditioned ales.

Reinheitsgebot: The Bavarian Purity Law, passed in Bavaria, in 1516, which stated that beer could only contain water, malted barley and hops. When yeast was discovered as a key ingredient in the brewing process, the law was amended to include it.

retronasal olfaction: The process by which aromas reach the receptors in the nasal cavity from the mouth through the back of the throat—as opposed to orthonasal olfaction, which is when aromas enter through the nostrils.

robust porter: A style listed in both the BJCP and Brewers Association style guidelines. Descriptions vary but, as a general rule, this term designates a strong porter with bold roasted notes and, on occasion, a pronounced hop bitterness.

rye beer: Beer brewed with a percentage of rye. There are many stylistic variations within this designation.

sahti: A traditional Finnish brew flavoured with juniper berries.

second runnings: See **parti-gyle brewing.**

session: A British term referring to a social gathering during which many pints are consumed back to back. In this context, session beers are designed to contribute to the jovial atmosphere without causing unpleasant levels of intoxication.

sessionable: Well suited to drinking in quantity

(see also **session**). Usually refers to lower-alcohol beers.

skunky/skunked: Describes beer with an unpleasant, skunk-like aroma after exposure to light. Also known as "lightstruck."

smash beer: An acronym referring to a beer that is brewed using only one type of malt (single malt) and one variety of hops (single hop).

spontaneous fermentation: Fermentation without the deliberate addition of cultivated yeast.

SRM: Standard reference method—a scale by which the colour of beer is measured.

Steinbier: A beer brewed using the historical method of heating up the wort by throwing in hot stones instead of using an external heat source.

step mash: A mashing technique in which the water and malt pass through a series of rests, each of which occurs at a specific temperature.

Sticke Alt: A seasonal stronger version of the Düsseldorf Altbier style.

taste: A component of flavour, taste refers to elements that can be detected by the taste buds.

top-fermented beer: Ale.

warming: A sensation that often indicates a higher alcohol level. This warming sensation may be apparent upon first contact as the beer passes through the mouth and chest. Alternately, it may present itself as a flushing of the cheeks or a full-body sensation after a portion of beer has been consumed.

wet-hopping: The addition of fresh (as opposed to dried) hops to beer. Also referred to as fresh-hopping.

widget: A small, spherical device that is inserted in beer cans. Used specifically for beers that are infused with nitrogen, these widgets serve to agitate the beer as it is served.

wheat wine: A barley wine brewed with high percentage (50 percent more) of wheat malt.

wort: The sugar water that is extracted from the mash and boiled. It is during the fermentation process that the wort becomes beer. Pronounced "wirt," like "dirt."

Zwickelbier: See **Kellerbier.**

Coolship for spontaneous fermentation

The Beerology Evaluation Sheet

Beer _____   Name _____

Style _____   Date _____

APPEARANCE
Colour

STRAW	GOLD	AMBER	COPPER	DARK BROWN	BLACK

Clarity

BRILLIANT   VEILED   CLOUDY

Head

POOR   GOOD   PERSISTENT

NOTES _____

AROMA
Intensity

FAINT   STRONG

Balance

SWEET   SHARP

MALT AROMA ☐ GRAIN ☐ BREAD ☐ SWEET
☐ TOAST ☐ NUT ☐ CARAMEL ☐ TOFFEE
☐ CHOCOLATE ☐ COFFEE
HOPS AROMA ☐ EARTH ☐ FLORAL ☐ HERBAL
☐ SPICE ☐ RESIN ☐ CITRUS
OTHER ☐ FRUIT ☐ SKUNK ☐ CORN ☐ CHEMICAL

Impression

OFF   NEUTRAL   NICE

NOTES _____

FLAVOUR
Intensity

FAINT   STRONG

Balance

SWEET   BITTER

MALT FLAVOUR ☐ GRAIN ☐ BREAD ☐ SWEET
☐ TOAST ☐ NUT ☐ CARAMEL ☐ TOFFEE
☐ CHOCOLATE ☐ COFFEE
HOPS FLAVOUR ☐ EARTH ☐ FLORAL ☐ HERBAL
☐ SPICE ☐ RESIN ☐ CITRUS
OTHER ☐ FRUIT ☐ CORN ☐ CHEMICAL

Impression

OFF   NEUTRAL   NICE

NOTES _____

My evaluation sheet is designed to take drinkers through every step of the sensory evaluation and consideration, providing common descriptors in each category. The Beerology Evaluation Sheet can also be downloaded from the Beer Tasting 101 page of www.beerology.ca.

MOUTHFEEL
Body

LIGHT   MEDIUM   FULL

Carbonation

FAINT   LIVELY   EXCESSIVE

SENSATION
☐CREAMY ☐SLICK ☐DRYING ☐WARMING
☐PUCKERING ☐ASTRINGENT ☐CHALKY
☐MOUTHCOATING ☐PRICKLY

NOTES _____

FINISH
Length

SHORT   MEDIUM   LONG

Intensity

FAINT   STRONG

Balance

SWEET   BITTER

GENERAL IMPRESSION
Craftsmanship

BORING   EXCELLENT

Freshness

OFF   STALE   FRESH

Personal Taste

DISLIKED   LIKED

NOTES _____

_____

_____

_____

_____

Beer Flavour Wheel

The content of the Beer Flavour Wheel was developed in the late 1970s by the American Society of Brewing Chemists, along with the European Brewery Convention and the Master Brewers Association of the Americas. The goal was to identify, name and define a range of individual components and provide brewers with a set vocabulary to describe the many flavours in beer.

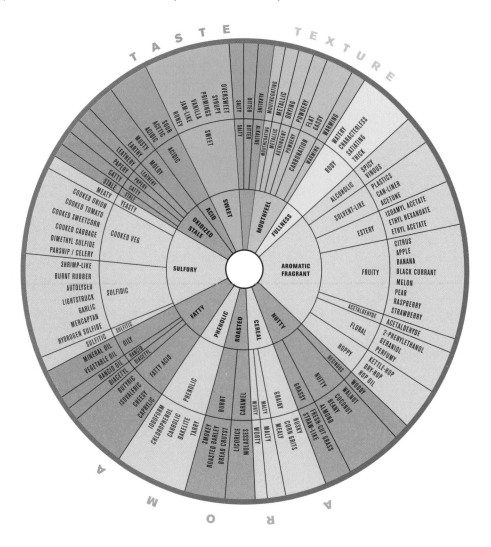

Adapted from the Beer Flavor Wheel, American Society of Brewing Chemists, St. Paul, Minnesota.

Ale vs. Lager

VISUAL REFERENCE CHARTS

These charts present some of the key information found in the Beer Styles part of this book, providing a visual comparison of different traits of the beers included in the Refreshing, Mellow, Striking and Captivating Brews chapters. Fruit and Spiced Beer as well as the beers in the Brews Beyond chapter have been omitted because they can be brewed in a wide range of styles and their traits vary greatly.

Style	Ale	Lager	Neither
Common Lager		x	
Lite Lager		x	
Pilsner		x	
Common Ale	x		
Cream Ale	x	x	
Kölsch	x		
Belgian Wheat Beer	x		
Bavarian Wheat Beer	x		
Märzen		x	
Dunkel		x	
Traditional Bock		x	
Doppelbock		x	
California Common		x	
Irish Red Ale	x		
English Brown Ale	x		
Stout	x		
Porter	x		
Baltic Porter	x	x	
English Pale Ale	x		
American Pale Ale	x		
Belgian Pale Ale	x		
English IPA	x		
American IPA	x		
Double IPA	x		
Berliner Weisse	x		
Lambic			x
Gueuze			x
Flanders Red-Brown Ale	x		
Saison	x		
Bière de Garde	x	x	
Dubbel	x		
Tripel	x		
Russian Imperial Stout	x		
Barley Wine	x		
Scotch Ale	x		

Alcohol by Volume

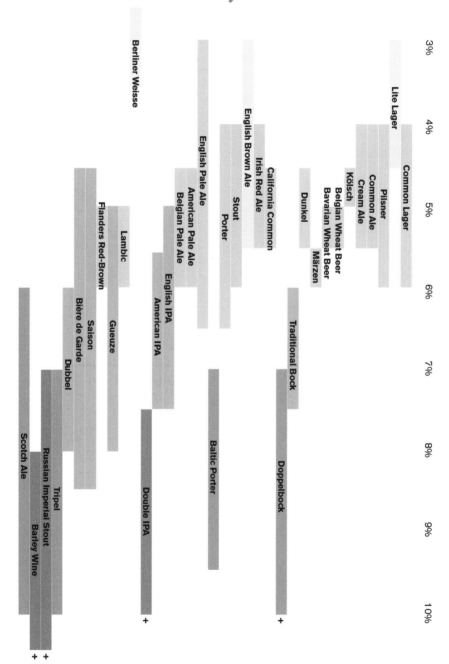

3%

Berliner Weisse

Lite Lager

4%

Common Lager

English Pale Ale

English Brown Ale

Pilsner
Common Ale
Cream Ale
Kölsch
Belgian Wheat Beer
Bavarian Wheat Beer

Irish Red Ale

5%

American Pale Ale
Belgian Pale Ale

California Common

Stout
Porter

Dunkel

Märzen

Flanders Red-Brown

Lambic

English IPA

6%

Bière de Garde

Salon

Gueuze

American IPA

Traditional Bock

7%

Dubbel

Baltic Porter

8%

Scotch Ale

Doppelbock

Tripel

Russian Imperial Stout

Double IPA

+

+

9%

Barley Wine

10%

+ +

Colour

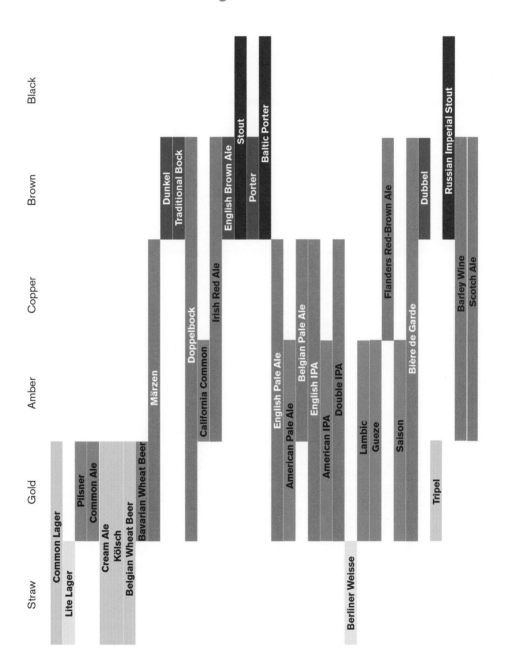

Straw — Gold — Amber — Copper — Brown — Black

- Common Lager
- Lite Lager
- Pilsner
- Common Ale
- Cream Ale
- Kölsch
- Belgian Wheat Beer
- Bavarian Wheat Beer
- Märzen
- Doppelbock
- California Common
- Irish Red Ale
- Dunkel
- Traditional Bock
- English Brown Ale
- Stout
- Porter
- Baltic Porter
- English Pale Ale
- American Pale Ale
- Belgian Pale Ale
- English IPA
- American IPA
- Double IPA
- Berliner Weisse
- Lambic
- Gueze
- Saison
- Bière de Garde
- Tripel
- Flanders Red-Brown Ale
- Dubbel
- Barley Wine
- Scotch Ale
- Russian Imperial Stout

Style Comparison Charts

These charts provide a visual overview of how the different styles of beers listed in the Refreshing, Mellow, Striking and Captivating Brews chapters compare to each other.

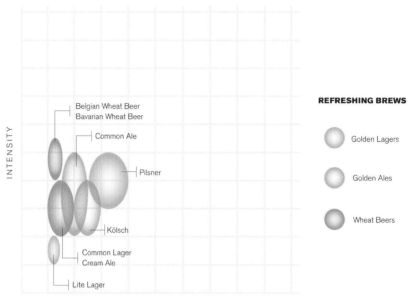

REFRESHING BREWS

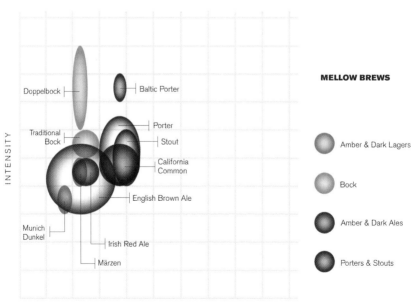

MELLOW BREWS

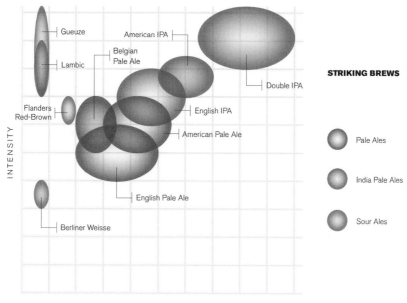

Gueuze

American IPA

Belgian
Pale Ale

Lambic

STRIKING BREWS

Flanders
Red-Brown

Double IPA

English IPA

American Pale Ale

INTENSITY

Pale Ales

India Pale Ales

Sour Ales

English Pale Ale

Berliner Weisse

BITTERNESS

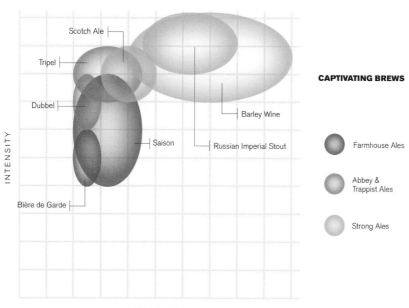

Scotch Ale

Tripel

CAPTIVATING BREWS

Dubbel

Barley Wine

INTENSITY

Saison

Russian Imperial Stout

Farmhouse Ales

Abbey &
Trappist Ales

Bière de Garde

Strong Ales

BITTERNESS

OTHER RESOURCES

Would you like to start brewing?

The Complete Joy of Home Brewing
    Charlie Papazian (Avon Books, 1984)

Dave Miller's Homebrewing Guide
    Dave Miller (Storey Publishing, 1994)

Designing Great Beers
    Ray Daniels (Brewers Publications, 1998)

How to Brew
    John J. Palmer (Brewers Publications, 2006)

Radical Brewing
    Randy Mosher (Brewers Publications, 2004)

Would you like to start cooking with beer?

The Best of American Beer and Food:
    Pairing and Cooking with Craft Beer
    Lucy Saunders (Brewers Publications, 2007)

The Canadian Craft Beer Cookbook
    David Ort (Whitecap Books, 2013)

Would you like to become a beer judge?

www.bjcp.org

Would you like to become a Certified beer server or Certified Cicerone?

www.cicerone.org

Are you looking for a comprehensive, technical beer reference book?

The Oxford Companion to Beer
    Garrett Oliver, ed.
    (Oxford University Press, 2011)

Acknowledgements

I'D LIKE TO START by thanking Meggie Macdonald, for hooking this up. A big thanks to my fantastic editor, Tim Rostron and everyone at Random House who worked on this project and, especially, Robert McCullough & Lindsay Paterson at Appetite by Random House whose advice and feedback greatly helped to shape this book.

I could not have gotten this far in my career without the support of my friends and family. In particular, I would like to thank Zoe Tarshis, Chris Moss and Danielle Dudycha for keeping me grounded during the course of this project.

A big shout-out to the following people for setting aside time to assist me with various aspects of this book: Adam Axbey, Dave Belle, Elvis Deane, Jabari Elliott, Gregory Hill, Joshua Hopkins, Susie Love, Jason Rees, Lauren Richard, Nicolas Rouleau, Andrea Rush, Sharon Shoot, Christine Sismondo, Zoe Tarshis, Jarvis Taylor and Nick Yeo.

Thanks the following suppliers for providing lovely things for us to photograph:

Bar Hop, Toronto ON
Brand Concepts,
         purveyors of quality beverage-ware
Chocolate by Wickerhead
Dairy Farmers of Canada

Huge thanks to the many brewers who have encouraged and assisted me in this delightful journey into beer; I'm glad to have this opportunity to share my passion for your products! I've learned so much from the numerous beer folk and food and drink specialists who have taken the time to share their knowledge with me over the years, and would like to thank the following people who answered specific questions that came up while assembling the information in this book:

Jan Adriaensens, Charlie Bamforth, Stephen Beaumont, Mike Buhler, Yvan De Baets, Ben Deschamps, Mark Carpenter, Vinnie Cilurzo, Frédéric Cormier, Martyn Cornell, Lorenzo Dabove, Ray Daniels, Roland Folz, Rudi Ghequire, Marina Gillis, Rob Gillis, Patrice Godin, Jérôme Goffinet, Rich Higgins, Lucy Joseph, Dave Kahle, Helen Knowles, Matthew Letki, Joel Manning, Chad McCarthy, Nathan McNutt, Iain McOustra, Stephen Morris, Ryan Morrow, Laurent Mousson, Manfred Newrzella , Simon Ogden, Charlie Papazian, Luke Pestl, Steve Polewacyk, Julia Rogers, Peter Salmond, Elfi Scheffers , Christine Sismondo, Willem Spannenberg, Chris Swersey, Martin Thibault, John Thompson, Joe Wiebe and Martin Zuber.

Finally, I wanted to acknowledge all of the people whose written work I consulted during my research: Charlie Bamforth, Stephen Beaumont, Christopher Bird, Peter Boucaert, Fritz Briem, Pete Brown, Paul KA Buttrick, Dick Cantwell, Vinnie Cilurzo, Martyn Cornell, Jack Curtin, Lorenzo Dabove, Ray Daniels, George DePiro, Bernard Dubrulle, Horst Durnbusch, Kristen England, Evan Evans, Tom Fitzpatrick, George Fix, Terry Foster, Rudi Ghequire, Brian Glover, Tim Hampson, Stan Hieronymus, Ian Hornsey, Ray Isle, Michael Jackson, Lee W. Janson, Nick R. Jones, Thomas Kraus-Weyermann, Joel Manning, Phil Markowski, Kurt Marshall, Burghard Meyer, Randy Mosher, Garrett Oliver, Charlie Papazian, Barrie Pepper, George Philliskirk, Pierre Rajotte, Gary Regan, Lucy Saunders, Conrad Seidl, Gary Spedding, Mitch Steele, Gordon Strong, Evan Rail, Gary Reineccius, Jeff Sparrow, Keith Villa, Thomas Vogel, Derek Walsh, Wayne Wambles, David Wondrich, Jamil Zainasheff and Michael Zepf.

Index

Abbey ale, 91–93
  dubbel, 92
  Patersbier, 94
  quadrupel, 94
  tripel, 93, 146
acetaldehyde, 150
Acetobacter, 77, 103, 150
acidity, 31, 67
  and barrel aging, 77
  and food pairing, 127–29
adjuncts, 6, 33, 150
aftertaste, 23
aging, 7, 77, 81, 89, 102–3, 153–54. *See also*
  cellaring
alcohol by volume, 113, 150, 160
alcohol content
  and beer cocktails, 140
  and food pairing, 126, 127, 129, 136
  visual reference chart, 158
  and warming sensation, 23, 136, 155
ales
  Abbey and Trappist, 91–93, 94
  Altbier, 155
  amber and dark, 56–60, 135
  American amber, red and brown, 56–60
  American IPA, 74
  American pale, 70, 136, 145
  barley wine, 87, 97
  Belgian pale, 71
  Belgian strong, 99